THE MOTHERS IN FAUST

12/16/81

THE MOTHERS IN **FAUST**

THE MYTH OF TIME AND CREATIVITY

HAROLD JANTZ

THE JOHNS HOPKINS PRESS: BALTIMORE

CONTENTS

THE MOTHERS IN FAUST

One of the most pursued and most elusive mysteries in the whole of Goethe's *Faust* is the meaning and intent of the realm of the Mothers to which the hero goes and from which he returns with the images of Helen and Paris. The many explications proposed hitherto are widely different, sometimes discrepant, even mutually exclusive. Can the scene, as Goethe wrote it, be all that ambiguous, or does the difficulty perhaps lie in the alien interpretations to which this scene has been subjected? As will appear, the latter is more likely to be the case: most of the past attempts at solution have been philosophical-intellectual, whereas we know from Goethe himself that this scene, like the *Faust* in general, is symbolical-pictorial, a configuration that does not arise out of an abstract idea and cannot be reduced to it. The discrepant results in its interpretation arise from discrepant points of view and basic premises introduced by alien ideological systems. Each of them is a bed of Procrustes into which the scene is forced, by stretching or cropping, and made to fit, more or less. With the great riches the scene contains, almost every premise and approach can find some feature that can be made to fit after a certain amount of manipulation, so long as one does not go back to the text. When one does, one sees how many features have been suppressed or overlooked, often precisely those features that provide the main support for another explication based on a different premise and approach.

In sum, the ambiguities of this scene are not inherent in it: they are usually imposed on it from without. However, in the few attempts at an intrinsic approach, based purely on the text, quite discrepant results have also been attained. This happens not only because ideological biases manage to intrude inconspicuously, in spite of sincere efforts to keep them out, but also because the scene itself remains ambiguous if studied in isolation or in narrower context. This is to be expected and is in accordance with common literary and human experience. Everyone has observed how a phrase or a sentence or a paragraph, obscure or ambiguous by itself, may become reasonably clear when seen in its larger context. A dramatic scene of this complexity would all the more stand in need of a larger context for its clarification and right under-standing—not merely the immediate context of the nearby scenes obviously connected with it, but the larger context of the whole drama in which it is clearly a key scene.

Just this broader view has been lacking in all the explications to date, and one cannot except those interpretations that have turned to the rest of the drama simply for select passages that would confirm already fixed and precon-ceived notions. They merely indulge in an expanded kind of Procrusteanism. The one partial exception, an interpretation that viewed this scene as one manifestation in a larger symbolic context, will be the concern of the third chapter of this study.

Any such opening of wider perspectives, from the context of the whole Faust drama, will progress far toward clarifying the scene. However, as is usually the case in the more difficult works of the great authors, one must go to the larger corpus of the poet's work for certain particulars, observing care-fully, for instance, the connotations habitually associated in his mind with certain indicant phrases or characteristic formulations. Astonishingly enough, this has never been done for the episode of the Mothers, except incidentally and sporadically, inadequately even for such an obvious favorite Goetheanism as "Gestaltung, Umgestaltung," "formation, transformation," and not at all for the immediately preceding words:

> Die einen sitzen, andre stehn und gehn,   6286
> Wie's eben kommt.

> *Some sit, some stand, some wander to and fro,*   6286
> *As it may chance.*

This formulation, seemingly so casual, actually originated within the sphere of his aesthetic criticism and cannot correctly be understood apart from the larger Goethean context.

The contextual approach, however, must be an even broader one, for Goethe did not live and create in isolation. He was a master of the treasures of Western civilization and he made sovereign use of them for his purposes. The *Faust* is a product of this greater literary tradition and it cannot be adequately explained apart from it any more than can the *Aeneid* or the *Divine Comedy* or *Hamlet*. In each case, of course, the text itself must finally remain at the vital center of interest.

Thus, when one observes the central motifs of the Mothers scene occurring in the *Faust* and other works of Goethe at an earlier, even much earlier stage, one must begin to give serious consideration to the problems of the genesis and development of this scene, all the more since this development seems to have been largely of the subconsciously creative kind. And when these central motifs, in similar and variant configurations, are found in earlier works of world literature with which Goethe was well acquainted, it would be neglectful not to look into them more closely for whatever light they may shed on the further symbolic extensions of this scene. Goethe himself pointed to Plutarch, but none of the commentaries ever did more than quote the brief passage from the life of Marcellus on the Mothers as goddesses at Engyon (the other passage sometimes quoted from another work offers an interesting supplement). Once again, the mere text as quoted will tell us little, but the larger context of the life of Marcellus will tell us much. I present it here for the first time, as I do also an entirely overlooked account of the Mothers of Engyon that Goethe found in another ancient author. Critics have been so busy putting things into Goethe that they have not had time to find out what was actually in Goethe.

Just as important as the literary stimuli and perhaps even more important in the genesis of this scene were the artistic stimuli to which several larger and smaller sections of this study are devoted, again for the first time. Since this scene is a product of the symbolic-pictorial imagination, it is fitting to allow the whole episode to remain myth and symbol and representation, to refrain from a course which would reduce it to mere philosophical or allegorical terms, or worse, reduce it to some modern critical fashion or system of interpretation. It has its own structure, and no extraneous structure should be imposed upon it.

This study then is concerned with configurations, with structures. The structures with which it is concerned are the intrinsic literary-artistic structures, not analogous structures, with points of reference outside literature, whether in philosophy, psychology, anthropology, linguistics, or whatever other intruding disciplines have presumed to tell poetry what it means.

A structure, if it exists, is never separable from its materials; indeed, the materials are an important element in the nature of the structure, as Goethe himself observed on a number of occasions [1] and not only Goethe. If, therefore, this is the first attempt at an intrinsically literary elucidation, it is inevitable that new materials will be brought to light. It is also inevitable that those for whom the old categories are compulsive will think of these as new "sources." This can be quite harmless if one keeps in mind that wherever new sources and parallels come to light in the course of this investigation, they do so incidentally as the result of the application of a new method to an old problem. In other words, though it may be interesting, even important to know the elements of Goethe's creative synthesis, the essential matter is to understand the final configuration as it exists in the total context of the Faust drama. Seeing and understanding that structural configuration is the aim and purpose of this study.

For a study of this nature nothing is more essential than the text itself. Just as important as the text is the context, and that means the whole of the *Faust*, in which this scene occurs almost exactly at the middle, only slightly beyond it. The text itself can be examined here in detail; not so the context, since the whole of it consists of over twelve thousand lines. The most important contextual passages can be cited and reviewed, but the isolated relevancies dispersed through the work must be left to the reader's knowledge of the whole and conscientious re-examination of its parts.

The introduction to the scene is ironic: though Mephistopheles is only too ready to use the carnival scene to introduce a "cure" for the financial woes of the empire, he becomes evasive when the emperor asks to see the figures of Helen and Paris. Faust has promised to produce them and turns to his usually masterful companion, but the latter suddenly appears to be a bit less than competent and has to explain why he is so, somewhat to his embarrassment. Whether or not the "rascal," as the Lord calls him, is feigning difficulties at this point must be decided from the total context. One cannot prejudge the matter on the basis of any cherished hypothesis or assumption. The evidence available outside the text is that Goethe, in an earlier summary of the action, explicitly stated that Mephistopheles lacked competence in the ancient world and has to employ other instrumentalities for entering into it.[2] Let us then watch the course of events in the order in which they happen. Here is the German original together with an English translation.[3]

FINSTERE GALERIE

MEPHISTOPHELES

 Was ziehst du mich in diese düstern Gänge?
 Ist nicht da drinnen Lust genug,
 Im dichten, bunten Hofgedränge   6175
 Gelegenheit zu Spaß und Trug?

FAUST

 Sag' mir das nicht, du hast's in alten Tagen
 Längst an den Sohlen abgetragen;
 Doch jetzt dein Hin- und Widergehn
 Ist nur, um mir nicht Wort zu stehn.   6180
 Ich aber bin gequält zu tun:
 Der Marschalk und der Kämmrer treibt mich nun.
 Der Kaiser will, es muß sogleich geschehn,
 Will Helena und Paris vor sich sehn;
 Das Musterbild der Männer so der Frauen   6185
 In deutlichen Gestalten will er schauen.
 Geschwind ans Werk! ich darf mein Wort nicht brechen.

MEPHISTOPHELES

 Unsinnig war's, leichtsinnig zu versprechen.

FAUST

 Du hast, Geselle, nicht bedacht,
 Wohin uns deine Künste führen;   6190
 Erst haben wir ihn reich gemacht,
 Nun sollen wir ihn amüsieren.

MEPHISTOPHELES

 Du wähnst, es füge sich sogleich;
 Hier stehen wir vor steilern Stufen,
 Greifst in ein fremdestes Bereich,   6195
 Machst frevelhaft am Ende neue Schulden,
 Denkst Helenen so leicht hervorzurufen
 Wie das Papiergespenst der Gulden.—
 Mit Hexen-Fexen, mit Gespenst-Gespinsten,
 Kielkröpfigen Zwergen steh' ich gleich zu Diensten;   6200

A Dark Gallery

MEPHISTOPHELES

> *Why draw me into these dark passageways?*
> *In there, is there not sport enough*
> *Amid the courtiers' whirling maze,*   6175
> *A chance for pleasantry and bluff?*

FAUST

> *Don't tell me that. In your old days did you*
> *Long since wear out the sole of that old shoe.*
> *But now your going to and fro*
> *Is only to evade, I know.*   6180
> *I am harassed to get things done,*
> *Marshal and Chamberlain urge me on.*
> *The Emperor wills it, he would presently*
> *Helen and Paris here before him see,*
> *Of man and womankind the primal mold*   6185
> *In figure manifest he wishes to behold.*
> *Quick, to the task. I may not break my word.*

MEPHISTOPHELES

> *So carelessly to promise was absurd.*

FAUST

> *You have, fine fellow, not reflected*
> *Just where your arts would lead us to.*   6190
> *First we have made him wealthy, true,*
> *Now to amuse him we're expected.*

MEPHISTOPHELES

> *You think it's easy to arrange,*
> *But here we stand at steeper stairs.*
> *You reach into a realm most strange*   6195
> *And rashly in the end make further debt.*
> *To summon Helen you think a light affair*
> *The way the paper phantoms gold did net.—*
> *Of witches' stitches and of specter's vectors*
> *And goitered dwarves I am a good effecter.*   6200

Doch Teufels-Liebchen, wenn auch nicht zu schelten,
Sie können nicht für Heroinen gelten.

FAUST

Da haben wir den alten Leierton!
Bei dir gerät man stets ins Ungewisse.
Der Vater bist du aller Hindernisse,   6205
Für jedes Mittel willst du neuen Lohn.
Mit wenig Murmeln, weiß ich, ist's getan;
Wie man sich umschaut, bringst du sie zur Stelle.

MEPHISTOPHELES

Das Heidenvolk geht mich nichts an,
Es haust in seiner eignen Hölle;   6210
Doch gibt's ein Mittel.

FAUST

                        Sprich, und ohne Säumnis!

MEPHISTOPHELES

Ungern entdeck' ich höheres Geheimnis.—
Göttinnen thronen hehr in Einsamkeit,
Um sie kein Ort, noch weniger eine Zeit;
Von ihnen sprechen ist Verlegenheit.   6215
Die M ü t t e r sind es!

FAUST (aufgeschreckt)
                        Mütter!

MEPHISTOPHELES

                        Schaudert's dich?

FAUST

Die Mütter! Mütter!— 's klingt so wunderlich!

MEPHISTOPHELES

Das ist es auch. Göttinnen, ungekannt
Euch Sterblichen, von uns nicht gern genannt.
Nach ihrer Wohnung magst ins Tiefste schürfen;   6220
Du selbst bist schuld, daß ihrer wir bedürfen.

FAUST

Wohin der Weg?

But devils' darlings, though they're not amiss,
Could hardly pass for heroines like this.

FAUST

Here is the same old hurdy-gurdy play.
With you one always gets into confusion.
You are the father of all occlusion,   6205
For every remedy you want new pay.
With but a muttered charm I know it's done,
One glances round, they're present at your spell.

MEPHISTOPHELES

The pagan folk I'd rather leave alone,
They dwell apart in their own hell.   6210
Yet there's a way.

FAUST

                        Tell me, without delay.

MEPHISTOPHELES

Loath am I higher mystery to display.—
Enthroned are goddesses in solitude sublime,
Around them is no place, still less a time;
Merely to speak of them I'd fain decline.   6215
They are the Mothers!

FAUST (startled)

                        Mothers!

MEPHISTOPHELES

                        You're afeard?

FAUST

The Mothers! Mothers! It sounds so strangely weird.

MEPHISTOPHELES

Yes, that it does. Goddesses unfamed
Unto you mortals, by us not gladly named.
To deepest depths you'll delve unto their dwelling,   6220
That we must seek them out your fault's compelling.

FAUST

Whereto the path?

MEPHISTOPHELES

    Kein Weg! Ins Unbetretene,
  Nicht zu Betretende; ein Weg ans Unerbetene,
  Nicht zu Erbittende. Bist du bereit?—
  Nicht Schlösser sind, nicht Riegel wegzuschieben,   6225
  Von Einsamkeiten wirst umhergetrieben.
  Hast du Begriff von Öd' und Einsamkeit?

FAUST

  Du spartest, dächt' ich, solche Sprüche;
  Hier wittert's nach der Hexenküche,
  Nach einer längst vergangnen Zeit.   6230
  Mußt' ich nicht mit der Welt verkehren?
  Das Leere lernen, Leeres lehren?—
  Sprach ich vernünftig, wie ich's angeschaut,
  Erklang der Widerspruch gedoppelt laut;
  Mußt' ich sogar vor widerwärtigen Streichen   6235
  Zur Einsamkeit, zur Wildernis entweichen
  Und, um nicht ganz versäumt, allein zu leben,
  Mich doch zuletzt dem Teufel übergeben.

MEPHISTOPHELES

  Und hättest du den Ozean durchschwommen,
  Das Grenzenlose dort geschaut,   6240
  So sähst du dort doch Well' auf Welle kommen,
  Selbst wenn es dir vorm Untergange graut.
  Du sähst doch etwas. Sähst wohl in der Grüne
  Gestillter Meere streichende Delphine;
  Sähst Wolken ziehen, Sonne, Mond und Sterne——   6245
  Nichts wirst du sehn in ewig leerer Ferne,
  Den Schritt nicht hören, den du tust,
  Nichts Festes finden, wo du ruhst.

FAUST

  Du sprichst als erster aller Mystagogen,
  Die treue Neophyten je betrogen;   6250
  Nur umgekehrt. Du sendest mich ins Leere,
  Damit ich dort so Kunst als Kraft vermehre;
  Behandelst mich, daß ich, wie jene Katze,
  Dir die Kastanien aus den Gluten kratze.

MEPHISTOPHELES

            No path! Unto untrodden way,
  Not to be trodden, a path to the unseekable, nay,
  Not to be sought. Are you in mood?
  There are no locks, no bolts to push aside.   6225
  By loneliness will you be driven far and wide.
  Have you a concept of the void and solitude?

FAUST

  I think you might spare me such chatter,
  This sounds like witch's kitchen patter
  From a remote and vanished time.   6230
  Did I not traffic in world's vanity?
  Learn things inane, and teach inanity?
  If I spoke rightly, true to my conviction,
  Then doubly loud resounded contradiction.
  And when from hostile malice fled   6235
  To solitude and wilds I went instead,
  And, not to live alone and all forsaken,
  Unto the devil I have myself betaken.

MEPHISTOPHELES

  And even if you had swum through the ocean,
  With limitless expanse from your position,   6240
  Yet would you see there wave on wave in motion,
  Even as you shuddered at your near perdition.
  You would see something, in the watery green
  Of quiet seas the gliding dolphin see,
  See clouds drift by, see sun and moon and star.   6245
  Naught will you see in th'ever void afar,
  Nor hear your footfall as you stride,
  Nor find firm ground on which to bide.

FAUST

  You speak, of mystagogues the foremost quite,
  Who ever cheated trustful neophyte,   6250
  Only reversed: you send me to the void
  For growth of art and power there employed,
  Manipulate me like that cat, that I
  For you the chestnuts from the coals may pry.

Nur immer zu! wir wollen es ergründen, 6255
In deinem Nichts hoff' ich das All zu finden.

MEPHISTOPHELES

Ich rühme dich, eh' du dich von mir trennst,
Und sehe wohl, daß du den Teufel kennst;
Hier diesen Schlüssel nimm.

FAUST

Das kleine Ding!

MEPHISTOPHELES

Erst faß ihn an und schätz ihn nicht gering. 6260

FAUST

Er wächst in meiner Hand! er leuchtet, blitzt!

MEPHISTOPHELES

Merkst du nun bald, was man an ihm besitzt?
Der Schlüssel wird die rechte Stelle wittern,
Folg ihm hinab, er führt dich zu den Müttern.

FAUST (schaudernd)

Den Müttern! Trifft's mich immer wie ein Schlag! 6265
Was ist das Wort, das ich nicht hören mag?

MEPHISTOPHELES

Bist du beschränkt, daß neues Wort dich stört?
Willst du nur hören, was du schon gehört?
Dich störe nichts, wie es auch weiter klinge,
Schon längst gewohnt der wunderbarsten Dinge. 6270

FAUST

Doch im Erstarren such' ich nicht mein Heil,
Das Schaudern ist der Menschheit bestes Teil;
Wie auch die Welt ihm das Gefühl verteure,
Ergriffen, fühlt er tief das Ungeheure.

MEPHISTOPHELES

Versinke denn! Ich könnt' auch sagen: steige! 6275
's ist einerlei. Entfliehe dem Entstandnen
In der Gebilde losgebundne Reiche!
Ergetze dich am längst nicht mehr Vorhandnen;
Wie Wolkenzüge schlingt sich das Getreibe,
Den Schlüssel schwinge, halte sie vom Leibe! 6280

Ah well, go on. We'll probe this ground,   6255
For in your naught my all may yet be found.

MEPHISTOPHELES
I do commend you ere you part from me,
You understand the devil, that I see.
Here, take this key with you.

FAUST
                                        That little thing!

MEPHISTOPHELES
Take hold of it without disparaging.   6260

FAUST
It shines and flashes, grows within my hand.

MEPHISTOPHELES
How great its worth will you now understand?
The key will sense the right place from all others,
Follow it down, 'twill lead you to the Mothers.

FAUST *(shuddering)*
The Mothers! like a shock it smites my ear.   6265
What's in the word that I don't like to hear?

MEPHISTOPHELES
So limited in mind? by each new word disturbed?
Would you hear only what you've always heard?
Let naught perturb, however strange it rings,
You long accustomed to most wondrous things.   6270

FAUST
In apathy I see no weal for me,
The thrill of awe is man's best quality.
Whatever toll the world lays on his sense,
Enthralled, man deeply senses the immense.

MEPHISTOPHELES
Descend then! I could also say: ascend!   6275
It's all the same. Escape from the created
Into the unbound realms of forms,
Delight in what long since was dissipated.
Like coursing clouds the throng is coiling round,
Brandish the key and keep them out of bound.   6280

FAUST (*begeistert*)

 Wohl! fest ihn fassend fühl' ich neue Stärke,
 Die Brust erweitert, hin zum großen Werke.

MEPHISTOPHELES

 Ein glühnder Dreifuß tut dir endlich kund,
 Du seist im tiefsten, allertiefsten Grund.
 Bei seinem Schein wirst du die Mütter sehn,   6285
 Die einen sitzen, andre stehn und gehn,
 Wie's eben kommt. Gestaltung, Umgestaltung,
 Des ewigen Sinnes ewige Unterhaltung.
 Umschwebt von Bildern aller Kreatur,
 Sie sehn dich nicht, denn Schemen sehn sie nur.   6290
 Da faß ein Herz, denn die Gefahr ist groß,
 Und gehe grad' auf jenen Dreifuß los,
 Berühr ihn mit dem Schlüssel!

(*Faust macht eine entschieden gebietende Attitüde mit dem Schlüssel*)

MEPHISTOPHELES (*ihn betrachtend*)

        So ist's recht!
 Er schließt sich an, er folgt als treuer Knecht;
 Gelassen steigst du, dich erhebt das Glück,   6295
 Und eh' sie's merken, bist mit ihm zurück.
 Und hast du ihn einmal hierher gebracht,
 So rufst du Held und Heldin aus der Nacht,
 Der erste, der sich jener Tat erdreistet;
 Sie ist getan, und du hast es geleistet.   6300
 Dann muß fortan, nach magischem Behandeln,
 Der Weihrauchsnebel sich in Götter wandeln.

FAUST

 Und nun was jetzt?

MEPHISTOPHELES

       Dein Wesen strebe nieder;
 Versinke stampfend, stampfend steigst du wieder.

(*Faust stampft und versinkt*)

MEPHISTOPHELES

 Wenn ihm der Schlüssel nur zum besten frommt!   6305
 Neugierig bin ich, ob er wiederkommt.

FAUST (inspired)
>   Good, grasping it, I feel new strength arise,
>   My breast expands, on to the enterprise.

MEPHISTOPHELES
>   At last a glowing tripod tells you this
>   That you've arrived in deepest deep abyss.
>   You'll see the Mothers in its radiant glow,   6285
>   Some sit, some stand, some wander to and fro,
>   As it may chance. Formation, transformation,
>   Eternal mind's eternal recreation.
>   Girt round by images of all things that be,
>   They do not see you, forms alone they see.   6290
>   Do then take courage, for the peril's great,
>   And to that tripod do go forward straight
>   And touch it with the key.

(Faust assumes a decidedly commanding attitude with the key)

MEPHISTOPHELES (observing him)
>   Ah, that will do.
>   It joins and follows like a servant true.
>   Calmly you'll rise, raised by your fortune fair,   6295
>   Return with it before they are aware.
>   And once you've brought it hither, you can cite
>   Hero and heroine from out of night.
>   The first who ever will have dared this feat,
>   It's done, and yours will be the deed.   6300
>   Then must forthwith, to magic handling suited,
>   The incense cloud to gods become transmuted.

FAUST
>   And now what next?

MEPHISTOPHELES
>   Your being downward strain,
>   Sink with a stamp, and stamping rise again.

(Faust stamps and sinks)

MEPHISTOPHELES
>   I hope the key will help him well out yonder.   6305
>   Just whether he'll get back I rather wonder.

RITTERSAAL

. . . .

(Faust steigt auf der andern Seite des Proszeniums herauf)

ASTROLOG

    Im Priesterkleid, bekränzt, ein Wundermann,
    Der nun vollbringt, was er getrost begann.
    Ein Dreifuß steigt mit ihm aus hohler Gruft,
    Schon ahn' ich aus der Schale Weihrauchduft.
    Er rüstet sich, das hohe Werk zu segnen;   6425
    Es kann fortan nur Glückliches begegnen.

FAUST *(großartig)*

    In eurem Namen, Mütter, die ihr thront
    Im Grenzenlosen, ewig einsam wohnt,
    Und doch gesellig. Euer Haupt umschweben
    Des Lebens Bilder, regsam, ohne Leben.   6430
    Was einmal war, in allem Glanz und Schein,
    Es regt sich dort; denn es will ewig sein.
    Und ihr verteilt es, allgewaltige Mächte,
    Zum Zelt des Tages, zum Gewölb der Nächte.
    Die einen faßt des Lebens holder Lauf,   6435
    Die andern sucht der kühne Magier auf;
    In reicher Spende läßt er, voll Vertrauen,
    Was jeder wünscht, das Wunderwürdige schauen.

ASTROLOG

    Der glühnde Schlüssel rührt die Schale kaum,
    Ein dunstiger Nebel deckt sogleich den Raum;   6440
    Er schleicht sich ein, er wogt nach Wolkenart,
    Gedehnt, geballt, verschränkt, geteilt, gepaart.

. . . .

(Paris hervortretend, dann Helena)

FAUST

    Hab' ich noch Augen? Zeigt sich tief im Sinn
    Der Schönheit Quelle reichlichstens ergossen?
    Mein Schreckensgang bringt seligsten Gewinn.
    Wie war die Welt mir nichtig, unerschlossen!   6490

HALL OF THE KNIGHTS

. . . .

(Faust rises to view on the other side of the proscenium)

ASTROLOGER

> In priestly vestment, wreathed, a wonder man,
> Who now fulfills what boldly he began.
> With him a tripod from the crypt below,
> An incense fragrance from the bowl I trow.
> Now he prepares the lofty work to bless.   6425
> Henceforth there can be nothing but success.

FAUST *(majestically)*

> In your name, Mothers, you who have your throne
> In boundlessnesses, ever dwell alone
> And yet together. Around your heads there hover
> Life's images, astir, yet lifeless ever.   6430
> What once has been in radiance diurnal
> Is stirring there, for it would be eternal.
> And you allot them, powers of greatest might,
> Unto the tent of day, to vault of night.
> On some the gracious course of life lays hold,   6435
> Others are sought by the magician bold.
> Assured, in rich profusion he displays
> The marvels whereon each would like to gaze.

ASTROLOGER

> The glowing key has scarcely touched the bowl
> When over the scene the misty vapors roll,   6440
> First creeping in, cloudlike, they onward glide,
> Spread out, curl up, contract, unite, divide.

. . . .

(Paris appears, then Helen)

FAUST

> Have I still eyes? Are beauty's richest springs,
> Outpouring, deeply to my soul revealed?
> Most blessed prize my fearful journey brings.
> How empty was the world, closed shut and sealed!   6490

Was ist sie nun seit meiner Priesterschaft?
Erst wünschenswert, gegründet, dauerhaft!
Verschwinde mir des Lebens Atemkraft,
Wenn ich mich je von dir zurückgewöhne!—
Die Wohlgestalt, die mich voreinst entzückte, 6495
In Zauberspiegelung beglückte,
War nur ein Schaumbild solcher Schöne!—
Du bist's, der ich die Regung aller Kraft,
Den Inbegriff der Leidenschaft,
Dir Neigung, Lieb', Anbetung, Wahnsinn zolle. 6500

What is it since my priesthood was attained?
Worth wishing for, firm based and well sustained.
May all life's breath from me have waned
If I relinquish you, fail in my duty.—
The lovely form that once enthralled my sight   6495
And gladdened me in magic mirror light
Was but a foamy semblance of such beauty.—
To you I yield the pulse of all my forces,
The quintessence of passion's courses,
Desire, love, adoration, madness yield.   6500

CHAPTER ONE: THE CONFIGURATIVE APPROACH

It is important to remember, from the beginning, that this scene is primarily a product of the poetic imagination, not of the abstract intellect that only secondarily seeks poetic embodiment for its ideas. Unfortunately, even the so-called symbolic interpretations tend to be indefinite and conceptual; indeed, it is symptomatic that the interpreters never quote Goethe's very clear and succinct definition of a symbolic action, but only his longer, less precise ones. The philosophical approach to the mystery has always ended in failure and must necessarily do so, as Goethe himself warned. On the other hand, the configurative approach is far closer to Goethe's poetic processes as he himself saw them:

> *Altogether, it was not in my nature as a poet to strive to embody*
> *something abstract. I received impressions in my mind, impressions*
> *indeed of a sensuous, animated, lively, colorful, hundredfold kind,*
> *as an active imagination offered them to me. As a poet I had nothing*
> *more to do than round out and develop such views and impressions*
> *artistically in myself, and, by means of a lively representation, so to*
> *bring them to view that others might receive the same impressions on*
> *hearing or reading my delineation of them.*[4]

Though Goethe, here and elsewhere, insisted that the *Faust* is not a philosophical work and will not yield its meaning to a philosophical approach, he clearly did not mean that there was no philosophy, no thought, no reflection in it. The intellectual elements are plainly present and at a number of points they are important; at a few, such as the translation scene, they are centrally important. It would be as absurd to deny this as it has been absurd in past criticism to accord the philosophical approach a place of paramount importance. To be sure, it must be admitted that the highest degree of absurdity is reached when philosophical approaches are applied to the work that are anachronistic, even totally alien to it, as has happened from the days of German idealism to the days of German existentialism, and beyond. In those limited instances in *Faust* where the philosophical approach is relevant, it has to be the kind of philosophical approach that is germane to the work, to the author himself, and to the traditional materials and structures that he creatively incorporated into the work. To force the drama into some discordant philosophical attitude or system, however pretentious its claims to universal validity, is to commit Procrustean violence against it.

Heedless of Goethe, the philosophical approach continues to dominate, and his words of warning are ignored. Few of the past studies pay more than passing attention to the poet's pictorial imagination. As quickly as possible they brush aside the figures in order to reach the inner "meaning" and "idea." Would it not be more appropriate to try to see what it is that Goethe here represents in terms of the images, figures, and larger poetic configurations? Instead of trying to abstract some "meaning" from them, it would be more to the purpose to surround them with the full aura of connotations that they had for the poet, as they came to him through a long life of rich, vivid, varied impressions in artistic, poetic, scientific, psychological experience, presided over by the power of his sovereign creative imagination.

Though this study can reveal many of the elements that went into the final creative synthesis of the scene, the creative synthesis itself is Goethe's own, is unique, different from the synthesis that any other poet could have made, simply because so very much of Goethe's own experience and reflection went over into it, inevitably. It has been the fashion for the past century and a half to esteem only the inner creative processes and to dismiss the materials and structure as secondary, even inconsequential. How wrong-headed such an attitude seemed to Goethe, has been indicated and will later again be made evident. And there are further instances where he shows his understanding of the intrinsic importance of the traditional materials in the creative synthesis.

Vital to the procedure to be undertaken here is the symbolic approach; but it must be Goethe's own kind of symbolic approach, not an anachronistic one of a later date. His briefest and clearest definition of a symbolic drama, a symbolic action, occurs in his Shakespeare essay of 1813: ". . . eine wichtige Handlung, die auf eine noch wichtigere deutet," "an important action that points to an even more important one."[5] For the present inquiry this means first of all that it will not do to brush aside the outer action to get at the "real" meaning. The outer action is itself an important action, a real meaning, integral with the still more important action, the deeper meaning, to which it points, which it "signifies." It also means that the passages concerned with the Mothers cannot merely be analyzed (certainly not within the narrow limits of the "interpretative method"); they must be viewed as a whole within their

setting in the entire Faust drama, as text within context, and any theory, however brilliant, that goes contrary to the spirit of the whole, must be dismissed
as irrelevant.

The configurative method is structural in its approach, structural in an
intrinsically literary-artistic sense; it regards the whole as more than the sum
of its parts. Unlike the philosophical, ideological approach, it does not attempt
to abstract an idea from the complex of phenomena. Instead, it seeks out the
main lines of form and force, and accents them in order to make clear the
intricate complex of phenomena. It does not abstract or draw away from the
original image and try to explain it in another medium, in alien concepts; it
simply tries to find and strengthen the main contours of the original image and
thereby to explain it in its own terms and forms. In the same way it approaches
the larger complexes and actions. It avoids the disintegration of the analytic
approach by using the genetic and contextual approach and observing the
gradual growth and integration of an image complex up to its final realization
in the creative work of the poet.

A poetic process of this kind is relatively easy to trace and describe
when it takes place on a largely conscious level, as is the case with the larger
contours of Faust's last earthly activities in acts four and five, as I traced them
in "The Symbolic Prototypes of Faust the Ruler."[6] Far more difficult to trace
and describe is a poetic process which takes place on a largely subconscious
level, as in the present instance of Goethe's poetic integration of the realm of
the Mothers. That it is not impossible to trace is due to the fact that the subconscious creative processes frequently emerge in the course of their development; when one has learned to observe them, they will at times come to view
with startling clarity.

In the early stages a subconscious image complex may be and often is
rudimentary or incomplete even when the larger contours are already fore-
shadowed. Only as it grows, absorbs and integrates further image complexes,
throwing off whatever is not germane or assimilable, only as it approaches its
mature synthesis, does the whole attain to a greater clarity of inner forms as
well as outer contours.

Thus, if one thinks of these image complexes as the outer indicative
sign of the inner creative processes, one will understand them truly in their
context. If, however, one reverts, by superficial analogy, to older stereotypes
and thinks of these image complexes as further "sources" or "influences," one
will surely miss the point both of Goethe's poetic processes and of the configurative approach to them. In previous studies, before my Amsterdam address

of 1965, I felt it unnecessary to make this point.[7] For most readers it probably is unnecessary, but for the few with rigid categories and reductive impulses it would perhaps be well to make the point once more, in the hope that it may not be necessary to make it again.

The first image complex to be examined may serve to illustrate the difference. Taken naively as a "source" it would hardly be near enough in time or in detail to be convincing (even aside from the questionable basic assumption of such a "source"). Taken, however, as an early and rudimentary stage of an eventual configuration, it becomes meaningful and illuminating. The configurative approach, in sum, is not static but dynamic; it is concerned not with a fixed group of images but with an image complex as it develops and as it functions in the total action. The first necessary though tentative step leads into the ancient cave of time.

In a famous work on ancient and modern art, with which Goethe was well acquainted by 1772, there is a section devoted to a myth now nearly forgotten but once well known. The original Latin account is quoted at length together with a German translation. Here is an English version of the pertinent lines:

> *Far away, all unknown, beyond the range of mortal minds, scarce to be approached by the gods, is a cavern of immense age, hoary mother of the years, her vast breast at once the cradle and the tomb of time. . . . Before the entrance sits Nature, guardian of the threshold, of age immense yet ever lovely, around whom throng and flit spirits on every side. . . .*
>
> *When the Sun [Apollo] rested upon the spacious threshold of this cavern, Dame Nature ran to meet him. . . . The adamantine door swung open of its own accord and revealed the vast interior, displaying the house and the secrets of Time.*[8]

This Cave of Time is not necessarily the point of origin or inciting incident of Goethe's mythopoetic processes. It stands, however, in the main line of the poetic tradition about such a realm, so that Goethe would probably have come upon it variously in the normal course of his reading and not only in the one art book with its fascinating illustrations. Furthermore, we know that young Goethe played with the imagining of such a realm in at least one of his work, the "Götter, Helden und Wieland."[9]

The factual background is briefly this: in his library Goethe had the collected works on ancient and modern art by Joachim Sandrart, in the new edition of 1768–75, in eight volumes folio. To judge from the review of one volume in the *Frankfurter gelehrte Anzeigen*, October 13, 1772, he or his father had acquired the work at the time of publication.[10] However, he left it at home in Frankfurt when he went to Weimar, and only later, when the family library was dispersed in 1794, did he send for it, along with other books he wanted. His early review sharply criticized the new edition for the botchery of its engravings and in text also compared it unfavorably with the original editions. Just how early Goethe knew the original editions, which had appeared during the 1670's and 80's with a profusion of large and splendid engravings, is uncertain; possibly he had known them since childhood, probably not later than the time of his art studies with Oeser at Leipzig. Sandrart's works were evidently esteemed in their time and safeguarded, for to this day they have not become really rare.

The volume of Sandrart of chief concern in this instance is the *Jconologia Deorum, Oder Abbildung der Götter*, which first appeared at Nürnberg in 1680. There, after leafing through such preliminary matter as the panegyric to the *Fruchtbringende Gesellschaft* (its swan song, as it turned out) and arriving at the mythology proper, one comes upon a plate that attempts to illustrate the primordial chaos and then a second plate depicting the Cave of Eternity, the *Antrum Aeternitatis*. It would be futile to look in any modern mythology for Aeternitas as a primordial goddess, in vain even in the huge, seemingly all-inclusive Pauly-Wissowa *Real-Encyclopädie der classischen Alter-tumswissenschaft*. But in the older mythologies, from Boccaccio's *Genealogia Deorum* to those standard in Goethe's youth, Aeternitas is included, often as the first of the goddesses. The myth connected with her comes from the late Roman poet, Claudianus (*ca.* 400 A.D.), although he did not personify or name her; only later when *mater annorum* was seen as the subject rather than as in apposition to the subject *spelunca* was this "Mother of the Years" given the name *Aeternitas*. All this was undone by the critical scholarship dominant from the late eighteenth century to the present, and the myth itself so effectively consigned to oblivion that Goethe scholars have apparently remained unaware of it. Even Claudianus' description of Dame Nature, which has so many poetic echoes from the early Renaissance through Spenser to Goethe, seems to have disappeared from ken.

Sandrart, after the quotation from the second book of Claudian's poem on the consulship of Stilicho, continues with a paraphrase from the first chapter of Boccaccio's mythology which remained essentially the standard version and interpretation of the myth to Goethe's day. It stresses the symbol of the prolific matrix, its awesome remoteness, the cyclic issuance and return, the host of flitting souls. Accompanying all this, however, in Claudian and his followers, are features and details for which Goethe had no use, which, unmodified, would have impaired his own creative development of the myth: there is the ancient image of eternity in the circled serpent with tail in mouth, there is

the image of immutable law administered by the ancient man, there is the
image of the repository of the ages in the form of the four metals, there is the
adamantine gate and the visit of Apollo. The association of the last two with
the luminous key and the tripod would be dubious. However, a Goethean
association of the rich succession of engravings in Sandrart's volume with
Claudian's realm of all time, though hypothetical, would in a number of instances be suggestive, especially if it is understood that this process of assimila-
tion could hardly have been either conscious or immediate, and that these
illustrations would have been fused in the course of time within an imagination
as pictorial as Goethe's. Here are mother goddesses and worshipers,

> *Some sit, some stand, some wander to and fro,*   6286
> *As it may chance.*[11]

Here is a majestic man in priestly clothes among them. Here, furthermore, are
illustrations suggestive of images and scenes in the carnival, in the "Classical
Walpurgis Night," in the Helena act; and then there is the frontispiece, illus-
trating the cycle of life and time, through death and destruction to re-naissance.
However, the image complex of the Mother realm, still a matter of separate
motifs here in Sandrart, was at a later date to come before Goethe's eyes in a
single *eikon*.

Claudian's images of the "cavern of immense age, hoary mother of
the years, her vast breast at once the cradle and the tomb of time" and of
"Nature, guardian of the threshold, of age immense yet ever lovely" assume
a somewhat greater importance when it becomes clear how much they helped
shape the earlier sketches for the second part of *Faust*, before the final inspiration for the Mothers scene came to the fore and displaced scenes previously
planned. What remains from Claudian in the final version is the impression of
the awesome remoteness, of the spirits thronging and flitting on every side,
and the image of a repository of time. However, the great sibylline figure at
the entrance to the cave also remains in the completed work, in the "Classical
Walpurgis Night." Faust is brought to Manto, she welcomes him and leads
him down the darksome passageway to the realm of Persephone. Significantly,
the attributes of the mystery of time remain with Manto and are brought out
in her brief dialogue with Chiron, especially in her words:

> *Ich harre, mich umkreist die Zeit.*   7481
> *I stay, around me circles time.*

As will become clear in Chapter Five, the poet had good artistic reasons for abandoning his long-cherished plan to write a Persephone scene when the realm of the Mothers arose in him to supplant it. Nevertheless, much of the Persephone imagery (and also Demeter imagery) remains in the work, assimilated, often subliminally, to other parts of the action. That the sibyl and cave imagery was originally stronger and more central we can see at several earlier stages of the work, particularly in the two announcements of the Helena drama drafted in 1826.

In the first draft Goethe describes Faust's quest for Helena, no longer in the dissonant Northern environment, but "in den Bergklüften Thessaliens unmittelbar bei dämonischen Sibyllen," "in the mountain chasms of Thessaly directly among demonic sibyls."[12]

This episode is changed in the second, much longer draft and explained in greater detail. Chiron is transporting Faust:

> So descending they arrive at the foot of Olympus; here they come
> upon a long procession of sibyls, well over twelve in number. Chiron
> describes the first ones to pass as old acquaintances and commends
> his ward to the contemplative benevolent daughter of Tiresias, Manto.
> She discloses to him that the way to Orcus is about to open up . . .
> and they all descend in silence.[13]

In the realm of Persephone Goethe also provided for a repository of memory, but this was in the older tradition and quite different from his later poetic realization.

CHAPTER THREE: THE ETERNAL-WOMANLY

If the Sandrart *Iconologia* was a beginning, it was merely a beginning. Many years were to pass, many a further image, associative, confirming, extending, was to be added and subconsciously assimilated. Well along in the process Plutarch's evocation of the Mothers, goddesses at Engyon, seems to have moved to a central position and ordered all these elements into a creative synthesis. When the new poetic entity took form and life in Goethe, suddenly and unexpectedly it would seem, it may well have reverberated deep down in him with something like the primordial shudder that overcame Faust when he first heard the mysterious, disconcerting name. Thus, like a spontaneous creation touched off by the magic word in Plutarch, the myth of the Mothers assumed form in Goethe and function in *Faust*. It evidently took Goethe himself by surprise; the course of the creative process remained subconscious, and only the final formative achievement stood clearly before his consciousness. Thus he could say to Eckermann in all sincerity:

> *I can disclose nothing more to you, than that I found in Plutarch that there was mention in Greek antiquity of the Mothers as goddesses. This is all I owe to tradition, the rest is my own invention.*[14]

This statement is essentially true, though it does not justify imputing to Goethe any belief in a *creatio ex nihilo*, a belief which to him was an aesthetic fallacy. He himself, as the Timoleon-Faust study indicates,[15] emphatically rejected such a possibility, blamed the vagueness and emptiness of many a poetic effort on this fallacy, and himself had deep respect for the substance, the "Stoff," as a partner in artistic creation. In some instances he remained consciously aware of the origins and course of the creative process and was able to give an account of it, even when it extended over decades, as in the case of the "Paria" or of the Helena act.[16] In other instances, as in the present one, the process remained largely or wholly subconscious. If it did so, what evidence is there that it took place over so long a span of time, that he did not simply make up the scene completely in late 1829 and early 1830 when he came to that part of *Faust* where he needed it? The evidence, derived from repeated observation, indicates that the subconscious does come to the surface every so often and leaves unmistakable traces of its presence. Its presence can be perceived in related motifs within the drama itself, from its earliest passages onward.

The imagery of the realm of the Mothers, far from being isolated and unique, is to be found in constant transformation throughout the drama, from beginning to end. In the very first poetic part, the lyric "Dedication," the themes of the mystery of time and the mystery of creativity are announced, and in the concluding *Chorus Mysticus* we hear of the symbolic nature of that which happens in the realm of time, of imperfect creative effort finally realized, and of the principle of the eternal-womanly that draws us onward. To be sure, the final chorus is not generally interpreted this way; indeed, the last two lines are usually explained in a sentimental idealistic way that has little to do with the last scene and almost nothing with the drama as a whole. Like the passages on the Mothers, the last chorus also has suffered from being interpreted in isolation and out of context. Once we study these and cognate passages in their total context, all such splintering, sundering interpretations can be eliminated.[17]

Let us then survey the passages in *Faust* where Goethe is concerned with the principle of the feminine, examining them singly and in their totality. The very first monologue of Faust already brings such a passage, though it may at first seem to be out of harmony with the concluding statement. As will become clear, also from comparison with several early poems, young Goethe was using traditional symbolic language here within an established frame of reference. Thus understood, the first passage fits very well with those that follow. Indeed, the feminine images with a positive relation to Faust will be seen to form a unity and continuity throughout the drama: the vision of the beautiful woman in the magic mirror, Margarete, the Mater dolorosa, the Mothers, Helena, Galatea, the Mater gloriosa.

The union is, to be sure, the ancient and Renaissance union or fusion of pagan and Christian imagery. With this in mind, the great image of nature as *mater* and *nutrix* in the first monologue in the *Faust* is one of nobility and significance:

> Wo fass' ich dich, unendliche Natur? 455
> Euch Brüste, wo? Ihr Quellen alles Lebens,
> An denen Himmel und Erde hängt,
> Dahin die welke Brust sich drängt—
> Ihr quellt, ihr tränkt, und schmacht' ich
>   so vergebens?

Where shall I seize on you, O endless nature,   455
And where, you breasts, you sources of all life,
On which both heaven and earth depend,
Toward which our withered hearts extend,
You flow, you feed, and I pine thus in vain?

This represents, of course, a very ancient and widely popular symbolic complex, as has been suggested in Chapter Two. In this tradition are the words of Friar Lawrence in his first speech in Shakespeare's *Romeo and Juliet*, referring to nature as a nourishing mother (II.iii):

And from her womb children of divers kind
We sucking on her natural bosom find,

or the cognate words of Timon of Athens (IV.iii):

Common mother, thou,
Whose womb unmeasurable, and infinite breast,
Teems, and feeds all,

or more amply, the description of "Great Dame Nature" in the fifth and following stanzas of the "Mutabilitie" Canto VII at the end of Spenser's *Faerie Queene*, and numberless other poems of European literature which adopted this symbolism as an integral part of their poetic imagery.

To avoid old misunderstandings, and also to make clear the relation to the next image, it may be best to restate the obvious here: Nature is imagined as a woman who creates (gives birth) and sustains (gives nourishment). All living creatures are her children; it is tragic for them when they are cut off (or cut themselves off) from her love, and it is their strongest yearning to return again to the bosom of her sustaining love. In poetry, at any rate, it continued to be remembered that the original meaning of the word *natura* was birth. The eternal cycle of life and death was suggested by the image of creatures coming forth from her as from a womb and returning to her as to a grave. Young Goethe expressed such a nascent relation to nature most plainly and directly in the first version of "Auf dem See" (W.A. I, 1:387):

Ich saug an meiner Nabelschnur
Nun Nahrung aus der Welt.
Und herrlich rings ist die Natur,
Die mich am Busen hält.

Umbilically I now absorb
My sustenance from the earth.
Nature that holds me to her breast
With radiance is begirth.

Within the realm of this imagery the Renaissance artist meant also to symbolize nature when he depicted the body of a beautiful woman, and conversely he often painted an undulating fruitful landscape as a symbol of womanhood, as will appear in connection with the next image in *Faust*. With deep reverence the highest earthly form of this maternal nature was represented by the figure of the Madonna with the Infant Jesus at her breast. All this was held together in the bonds of symbolic unity: the love of man for woman is equated with the love of God (or of his visible representative, the sun) for all nature; the quickening power of his love calls forth her maternal abundance. The old theme of the year cycle, the love of Sol and Tellus, was a poetic commonplace. The specific instance of God's love came in the sending to mankind of His son who was born of the Virgin Mary.

Young Goethe in 1772 and 1773, in the period of the inception of *Faust*, showed quite clearly that he not only understood this ancient symbolic complex, but also that it was an integral part of his own poetic imagery. Passages from two poems in particular will illustrate this, "Der Wandrer" and "Künstlers Morgenlied." "Der Wandrer" indeed begins with the lines (W.A. I, 2:170):

Gott segne dich, junge Frau,
Und den säugenden Knaben
An deiner Brust!

Young woman, may God bless you
And the boy you nourish
At your breast.

That this young mother also stands for Nature itself blossoming forth in new uncomplicated life from the ruins of a past civilization becomes clear as this short poetic dialogue develops, and as the image of primordial family life (which is at the same time the image of the three of the Holy Family) emerges near the conclusion:

Natur! du ewig keimende,
Schaffst jeden zum Genuß des Lebens, . . .

Und du flickst zwischen der Vergangenheit
Erhabne Trümmer
Für deine Bedürfniß'
Eine Hütte, o Mensch,
Genießest über Gräbern!—
Leb wohl, du glücklich Weib!

Nature, ever prolific, you
Bear everyone to joy of living, . . .
And you, O man, among the splendid ruins
Of ages vanished
Will piece together
Unto your use a hut,
Rejoicing above graves.—
Farewell, O happy woman.

It is significant that Dürer, Altdorfer, and so many other Renaissance artists represented the Nativity, quite un-biblically, in a hut among architectural ruins. One era has died, another has been born. And by the way, the very scene of Goethe's poem, with a wanderer, a mother with suckling child, vegetation, and classical ruins, parallels the foreground of Giorgione's painting "The Storm."

Goethe explicitly adds the image of the Holy Mother and Child to this symbolic complex in a stanza near the end of "Künstlers Morgenlied" (W.A. I, 2:180):

Und sollst mir, meine Liebe, sein
Alldeutend Ideal,
Madonna sein, ein Erstlingskind,
Ein heiligs an der Brust.

And you, my love, will be to me
All meaningful ideal,
Madonna be, a first-born child
A sacred one at breast.

The utter paganism of the next three, concluding stanzas strikingly illustrates the point I made above. Young Goethe intended no impudence here as a "realistic" un-symbolical reading of the lines might suggest. His varied development of this set of images can be seen in such further poems as "Ein zärtlich jugendlicher Kummer," "Künstlers Abendlied," "Die glücklichen Gatten,"

"Einer hohen Reisenden," "Kore," "Metamorphose der Tiere," and the brief lyric drama "Künstlers Erdewallen"—to cite only a few instances from his early, middle, and late years. He tells us that even in his boyhood before he went to Leipzig he loved such pieces of ancient poetic wisdom as the Orphic hymns (W.A. I, 27: 12). In these hymns the symbolic synthesis of all the creative, procreative powers is a basic religious and poetic principle.

The image of the beautiful woman in the mirror that Faust sees in the "Witch's Kitchen" has traditionally and quite correctly been given its pictorial source in the "Venus" of Giorgione. It is only in recent decades, however, that there has been full recognition again of the conscious and intricate way in which the artist employed his pictorial symbolism. His Venus is reclining in the foreground against an undulating fruitful landscape which restates fully every contour of her body. Faust's enraptured words at the vision in the mirror show a full comprehension, show also an enrichment of sensuous connotation over the first monologue. Most important of all, they show a maturing from dependent child of Nature to active lover of Nature:

> Das schönste Bild von einem Weibe! 2436
> Ist's möglich, ist das Weib so schön?
> Muß ich an diesem hingestreckten Leibe
> Den Inbegriff von allen Himmeln sehn?
> So etwas findet sich auf Erden? 2440

> *A woman's image beauty enshrining!* 2436
> *Can woman, then, so lovely be?*
> *And must I find her body, there reclining,*
> *Of all the heavens the prime epitome?*
> *Can aught like this be found on earth?* 2440

The elevating, sublimating effect on Faust, so movingly expressed here, must be kept in mind and must be kept clear of Mephistopheles' degrading remarks if we are to understand what this image meant to Faust, what Goethe intended it to mean. It is deeply religious, albeit at the shrine of Venus. Anyone with an ear for the tone level of poetry and a sense of the continuity of imagery through the work cannot take seriously the Mephistophelean interpretation a few critics seem to favor here and in the Mothers scene. Only a fragmental approach and a merely cerebral reading could come to such results.

The abundant variety of forms that the feminine takes in the drama is intentional and significant. The most winsome and lovely of these forms, the most delicate and perishable, yet the most vital and perennial is Margarete. The motherhood for which she instinctively yearned became for her a mortal personal tragedy, as it did in a different manner for two other forms of the womanly who lost their children in death: the Mater Dolorosa, to whom Margarete in the "Zwinger" scene goes in her deepest despair, and Helena who is bereft of her son and of her will to live. The complete naturalness of Margarete, her fullness of life, the truth and rightness of her impulses, the tragic wrong which is the pitilessly ironic result, all this has a depth of symbolic import which is in part ineffable because its poetic creation went beyond the threshold of conscious art. Every reader feels its deep truth, though he will be at a loss to express it.

One factor in the ineffable is probably the ancient tragic wisdom of the cycle of life:

> Geburt und Grab,   504
> Ein ewiges Meer.
>
> *Birth and the grave,*   504
> *An infinite sea.*

Shakespeare particularly loved to call to mind the paradox that mother earth is both womb and grave, and young Goethe also variously expressed this dual function, as when he had the Savior address the earth in *Der ewige Jude*, as "Du Mutter, die mich selbst zum Grab gebar!" (W.A. I, 38:60). Likewise, Prometheus' explanation to Pandora of the mystery of Eros-Thanatos (W.A. I, 39:211–12) gives us this symbolic variant in renewed poetic power and seriousness, after it had been trivialized by a long succession of poets.

The ultimate, deep symbol of motherhood raised to the universal and the cosmic, of the birth, sending forth, death, and return of all things in an eternal cycle, is expressed in the Mothers, the matrices of all forms, at the timeless, placeless originating womb or hearth where chaos is transmuted into cosmos and whence the forms of creation issue forth into the world of place and time. As will be seen, a realm of this kind is more a matter of continuous poetic tradition than has ever been realized, and the relationship of this scene to other scenes in *Faust* is a close and manifold one. The Mothers are not only an essential element in the dramatic action, they are also an indispensable link in a vital symbolic series.

While Faust is in the realm of Persephone, the spectator accompanies Thales and Homunculus to the shore of the sea, the mother element of all life with its endless proteanism, over which reigns the successor of Aphrodite, Galatea, who is also called mother here (8386). The exultant paean of Thales after Galatea has passed in celebrant procession states the symbols in the form here appropriate of the life-giving and preserving waters (8433–37). Homunculus, who wishes to live truly and in the midst of life, organically embodied, not artificially separated by a glass wall, dashes his vial against the throne of Galatea, and in the highest exaltation of Eros flows out fiery into the womb of the sea from which he can be reborn in embodied form and rise upward in the scale of being:

> Und ringsum ist alles vom Feuer umronnen;   8478
> So herrsche denn Eros, der alles begonnen!

> *And all things around are immersed in the flame;*   8478
> *Let Eros prevail from whom everything came.*

This is closely related to the ninety-fifth Venetian epigram (W.A. I, 1:329):

> Du erstaunst und zeigst mir das Meer; es scheinet zu brennen.
>   Wie bewegt sich die Flut flammend ums nächtliche Schiff!
> Mich verwundert es nicht, das Meer gebar Aphroditen,
>   Und entsprang nicht von ihr uns eine Flamme, der Sohn?

> *You are astonished and point to the sea, it seems to be burning.*
>   *How the flood moves aflame round the ship in the night!*
> *Me it does not astonish, the sea brought forth Aphrodite,*
>   *Did not from her for us spring forth a fire, her son?*

Inevitably we think of those words of the Earth Spirit already quoted:

> *Birth and the grave,*
> *An infinite sea.*

Or we think of the words that Ovid has Pythagoras speak in the fifteenth book of the *Metamorphoses* (165, 255–57): "All things are changing; nothing dies." "What we call birth is but a beginning to be other than what one was before; and death is but cessation of a former state."

Faust had entered the realm of Persephone with the approval and aid of the perennially centered, indrawn, contemplative Manto, who is contrasted so pointedly with the ceaselessly active, outgoing, pedagogic Chiron. In space, Helena returns to her native Sparta and neighboring Arcadia, though in time she traverses (as Goethe several times remarked) "three thousand years" with Faust, on through the chief epochs of a new and different civilization, to the wedding of their two worlds and the tragically short life of their son. For Faust there remain the inalienable memories of transfigured life.

At the beginning of the fourth act, the representative figures of the womanly appear to him in the forms which the billowing cloud mantle assumes as it divides and floats away: Helen is one with her mother, Leda, and with the great Olympian mother, Juno; Margarete, as his first love, is associated with Aurora, the dawn. To the church fathers and mystics, Aurora was an epithet for the Mother of God, and Goethe associates the two in his commentary and verses on the twelfth idyl of "Wilhelm Tischbeins Idyllen." Herewith he provides a bridge to the concluding parts of the drama:

> *For just as in sacred pictures we see circles of little angel heads*
> *around the contenance of the transfigured Mother of God, heads*
> *that gradually dissolve in luminous cloudlets, just so are the roses*
> *intended here into which the red-fingered cloudlets of the morning*
> *dawn are meaningfully shaped. . . .*

> *When round Aurora, child divine,*
> *Roses in darkness are born to shine.*[18]

The words of Thales on the life-giving and preserving waters lead on to Faust's last earthly activity, his union with nature finally, his creative achievement of separating the waters from the land, his segregating of the fruitless and destructive attributes from the fruitful and sustaining ones, creating a nature which can, by eternal care, be kept a true *mater nutrix* of a free and strong mankind. Even as Thales in his exultant paean to the fertile sea omitted mention of its ominous opposite aspects (these the theme of Faust's indignation and resolution near the beginning of the fourth act), even so have I till this point omitted direct mention of the fact that Goethe also included figures in his drama that illustrate the grave negative aspects of the feminine as clearly as Mephistopheles does the negative aspects of the masculine in his active destructive impulses. Here again, on the negative side, the feminine figures occur in an abundant variety of forms: the witches in kitchen and on Brocken, Martha, the "virtuous" Lieschen, Lilith, the ladies at court, the Sirens, Lamias, and Phorkyads, the Trojan girls of the chorus, Eilbeute, and others— some of them committed to active evil, a few, like the Sirens, ambiguous, the rest merely limited and negative. From his youth onward Goethe was clearly aware of the negative and destructive in nature and on certain rare occasions he stressed its cruel terror.[19]

Faust, in his last earthly activity, centers his concern upon a nature in which land and sea are mixed in hapless chaos and mutually negate each other's fruitfulness. Here, however the negative aspect of the feminine, though potentially dangerous and destructive, is not actively evil, but on the contrary presents a creative challenge to a man of Faust's temperament. To restate the situation in the ancient, perennially recurring symbols of fairy tale, we have here the theme of the "perilous maiden," perilous to all but the destined hero who magically rescues the beautiful princess from imprisonment, awakens her to consciousness, cherishes and guards her as queen and mother of a restored and happy realm. Faust in this last wedding, with nature, has in a sense come full spiral to the object of his first yearning in the opening monologue, but now on the higher plane of achievement and fulfillment.

Since there may well be some misgivings about interpreting in feminine terms this nature which Faust creatively segregates, it should be pointed out that there is an exalted poetic prototype for this creative separation of land and sea, in which nature is most explicitly and elaborately described in feminine terms. The prototype occurs in the seventh book of Milton's *Paradise Lost* with its poetic exposition of the great act of divine creation. This creative act is symbolically re-enacted in human terms and on a human scale in Faust's last activity on earth. Here too we have no blasphemy or parody, but rather an old conviction (clearly found in Renaissance art theory and elsewhere expressed by Goethe) that man's creative activity is a symbolic restatement on a human level of the great act of divine creation. Milton's imagery (VII, 276–84) makes explicit what is implicit in Goethe's analogue:

> *The earth was formed, but in the womb as yet*
> *Of waters, embryon immature involved,*
> *Appeared not: over all the face of earth*
> *Main ocean flowed, not idle, but with warm*
> *Prolific humor softening all her globe,*
> *Fermented the great mother to conceive,*
> *Satiate with genial moisture, when God said*
> *'Be gathered now ye waters under heaven*
> *Into one place, and let dry land appear.'*

From here on the image of nature as a fruitful, nourishing mother is carried through consistently; in God's next act, creating vegetation, this is apparent both in His words of creation and in such details of the description as (317–19):

> *Then herbs of every leaf, that sudden flowered*
> *Opening their various colors, and made gay*
> *Her bosom smelling sweet.*

Likewise later, after God's command to the earth to bring forth animals, the narrating angel Raphael continues (543–46):

> *The earth obeyed, and straight*
> *Opening her fertile womb teemed at a birth*
> *Innumerous living creatures, perfect forms,*
> *Limbed and full grown.*

Goethe also took up the theme of the creative separation of the waters in the poetic aphorisms of his "Gott, Gemüt und Welt" (W.A. I, 2:216):

> Da, wo das Wasser sich entzweit,
> Wird zuerst Lebendigs befreit.

> Und wird das Wasser sich entfalten,
> Sogleich wird sichs lebendig gestalten;
> Da wälzen sich Tiere, sie trocknen zum Flor,
> Und Pflanzen-Gezweige, sie dringen hervor.

> > *There where the waters are separated,*
> > *The living is first liberated.*

> *And when the waters are unfolded,*
> *At once vitality is moulded;*
> *The animals wallow, they dry, they mature,*
> *And plants spring to branching and foliature.*

In Faust's realm also the creative act of dividing the land from the waters is followed by a teeming life upon the newly fruitful earth and by the cultivating-cultural work of man. Faust finally comes to a fully conscious realization and formulation of the specific end and purpose of what had started simply as a challenge to his creative and ordering impulse. In the last review of his realm he notes the danger from the threatening chaos outside the sea walls, but he realizes joyously that he has turned this also to the use and benefit of his realm, for the constant menace will keep the people alert and united, will prevent their degenerating in ease and security. Thus the negative feminine principle, like the negative masculine principle, is simply:

> Ein Teil von jener Kraft,   1335
> Die stets das Böse will und stets das Gute schafft.

> *Part of that force that would*   1335
> *Do evil evermore, and ever creates good.*

In nature around him Faust has achieved a resolution of this negative element. In himself he breaks its last ties by renouncing magic, courageously restraining himself from using a magic word to banish "Sorge" (Anxiety) from his presence. Thereby he lays himself open to her spite, and his blindness is the wound he carries off from his victory over her. She represents the last of the negative feminine elements, even as she had been the first to enter the drama, during Faust's reflections in his second monologue. The words accompanying his wish to renounce magic make his purpose completely clear:

> Stünd' ich, Natur, vor dir ein Mann allein,   11406
> Da wär's der Mühe wert, ein Mensch zu sein.

> *Nature, could I alone before you stand,*   11406
> *Then would it be worthwhile to be a man.*

Thus his last obligatory tie to Mephistopheles is broken, and he can now proceed to his glorious vision of a free people on a free soil, which arouses Mephistopheles' mordant malice and his impotent efforts to drag it all down to the level of an ironic jest.

Here again the failure to look at this scene in its larger symbolic setting and implications has led to some strange "modern" interpretations. Amusingly enough, these interpretations are based upon a ready credulity toward Mephisto's distorting words and deeds, accompanied by a hardened skepticism toward the Lord's words in the "Prologue" as well as toward Goethe's known attitude and intent.

Faust has now finally succeeded after many failures, many wrongs toward himself and others. The great good to the many inhabitants of his realm is his creative compensation for his several great wrongs; it is something positive, helpful, and constructive, whereas remorse would be only negative, futile, and destructive, as Goethe observed in one of his verse aphorisms (W.A. I, 2:249):

Nichts taugt Ungeduld,
Noch weniger Reue;
Jene vermehrt die Schuld,
Diese schafft neue.

No good in impatience,
Even less in remorse;
One increases the guilt,
The other is its source.

The new realm of his achievement is now "lebensfähig," capable of going on
independently toward the future life he envisions for it. His creative task and
masculine obligation toward this nature have been fulfilled, he is ready to enter
higher spheres of activity. Goethe presented the apotheosis of the active and
resilient man in the sketch for one of his "Episteln" (W.A. I, 5^2:371):

> der wackere Mann, der beständige,
> Der den Seinen und sich zu nutzen versteht und dem Zufall
> Klug sich beugt und groß dem Zufall wieder gebietet, ...
> Einen solchen habt ihr gesehen vor kurzem hinaufwärts
> Zu den Göttern getragen, woher er kam.

> *the valiant man, the intrepid,*
> *Who knows how to be useful to kin and to self, who discreetly*
> *Bows before chance and grandly again brings chance to subjection, ...*
> *Such a one in these recent days have you seen carried upward*
> *Unto the realm of the gods whence he came.*

The symbolism now used for the ascent to higher spheres is not that
of the Greeks and Romans, as Plutarch, for instance, outlined it: from the
sphere of "man" to the sphere of the "daemones," the sphere of the "heroes,"
and the sphere of the "gods." That religious complex has no adequate pro-
vision for carrying on one integral half of Goethe's symbolism. The Christian
complex, on the other hand, gives him full scope for the continuity of the symbolism to its ultimate expression. We must, however, beware of lightly assum-
ing that Goethe uses Christian symbol in a strictly Christian and orthodox
fashion. Here, as throughout the drama, syncrasy, harmonious amalgamation
remains his poetic-symbolic practice.

Let us look closely at all the feminine figures of this final scene and
note what aspects of the womanly they represent. The Virgin Mary is specifi-

cally designated as "Mater Gloriosa," that is, motherhood in heavenly glory. Beside her there is only the choir of penitent women, with the four singled out from the choir. Each of them expiated for (and removed) the negative elements with which she had been afflicted through human weakness or ignorance rather than active evil. The first is the sinner of whom Luke tells that she washed Jesus' feet with tears (an episode later assimilated to the Mary Magdalene legend). The second is the sinning Samaritan woman who gave Jesus to drink. The third is Mary of Egypt who atoned for her sinful life by her long eremitic repentance in the desert. The fourth is Margarete. All four have been grievously betrayed by instincts and impulses most natural to womanhood. The fulfillment of their life on earth in blessed motherhood had been tragically deflected and frustrated, and they now look up in adoration and for guidance to the one who had reached her ultimate fulfillment and sinless perfection, in becoming the mother of God. The last words of adoration addressed to her, by the Doctor Marianus, just before the "Chorus mysticus," are also a summation of the positively feminine in the drama:

> Jungfrau, Mutter, Königin,   12102
> Göttin, bleibe gnädig!

> *Holy Virgin, Mother, Queen,*   12102
> *Goddess, stay Thou gracious.*

What then is the "Eternal-Womanly" as Goethe unfolds it in the course of the drama? Is it the representation of divine grace and love? Is it the ideality which inspires to a sublimation of love, to an adoration which draws the spirit upward to higher spheres? That is what the critics by almost common consent have made it out to be, but how justly have they done so? At only a few points in the drama did that aspect of the feminine, ideality and power of inspiration, receive any emphasis. On the other hand, what was brought out again and again, in ever new form and expression, was the chief and perennial womanly attribute, namely motherhood with all that goes with it; and it is exactly this main aspect of womanhood which is extended symbolically to nature and to the creative matrix. Love, grace, ideality unfold from this central attribute.

The conventional interpretation has only limited relevance even for the concluding scene. What kind of womanly spirits do we find here in the company of the Mater Gloriosa? Had they on earth been the inspiration and uplifting power of any man? There is nothing about the three figures accompanying Margarete or about the whole choir of penitent women that can even faintly suggest this; and certainly if Goethe had intended his last lines to stress that factor in womanhood, it would have been his poetic duty to indicate it symbolically in the feminine figures he chose. Instead, he stressed what he had stressed throughout the drama: in the Mater Gloriosa, the bliss of highest maternal fulfillment; in the choir of penitent women, the sad factor of human fallibility, that the finest and truest impulse of womanhood could be deflected and frustrated, though also that these failings could be atoned for on earth and transcended in heaven. In the drama the actively masculine and the positively feminine striving toward self-fulfillment are both subject to the impairments of human failure, but never for this reason are they subject to the withdrawal of divine grace.

If we approach the problem from another angle, we come to the same results. What is the feminine principle in religion, in the Christian religion? At the very center of the process of salvation stands the doctrine of regeneration, of *rebirth*, without which salvation is impossible. Jesus' words to Nicodemus use that metaphor: "Except a man be born again, he cannot see the kingdom of God" (John 3:3). "Except a man be born of water and of the spirit, he cannot enter into the kingdom of God" (John 3:5).

The "Eternal-Womanly," therefore, was unmistakably intended by Goethe to comprise in symbolic form the great creative continuity of life, birth and rebirth in constantly renewed forms, the ultimate resolution of death, destruction, and tragedy in new cycles of life, constructive activity, and fulfillment. It is the abundantly fruitful, eternally replenished matrix of the fullness and recurrence of life, out of which the purposeful and constructive, conscious and active personality could arise and, with his task accomplished, return again to be reborn once more on a higher level. Meaningfully, in the last scene there is the chrysalis image with reference to Faust (11981–88), this an ancient symbol of resurrection, of rebirth in higher form. The "Eternal-Womanly," pregnant with the future, draws the heroic soul upward to a higher sphere of existence. Within this fuller context, this larger set of connotations, the final Chorus Mysticus takes on a more profound and appropriate meaning:

> Alles Vergängliche   12104
> Ist nur ein Gleichnis;
> Das Unzulängliche,
> Hier wird's Ereignis;
> Das Unbeschreibliche,

Hier ist's getan;
Das Ewig-Weibliche
Zieht uns hinan. 12111

All that is transient 12104
Is symbol mere;
The once deficient
Is realized here;
The indescribable
Here it is done;
The Ever-Womanly
Draweth us on. 12111

This realization of the symbolic nature of truth is beautifully expressed in the initial sentence of an entirely different work of Goethe's, the "Versuch einer Witterungslehre" of 1825:

The true, identical with the divine, can never be known to us directly. We behold it only in the reflection, in the instance, the symbol, in single and related phenomena; we become aware of it as incomprehensible life and yet cannot relinquish the wish to comprehend it after all.[20]

In the increasing understanding of Goethe's masterpiece one must not concentrate too exclusively upon the masculine "Faustian" principle; the feminine maternal principle also runs through it from beginning to end, and the poet gives it the high tribute of ultimate statement in his work. When the fuller content of his symbol of the "Eternal-Womanly" is perceived, the closing lines attain to a loftier dignity and become the adequately concluding summation not merely for the last scene but for the entire drama. One can also return with new insights to the central scene with which this study is concerned.

CHAPTER FOUR: THE MOTHERS AT ENGYON AND ELSEWHERE

Now that this central scene has been viewed within the larger context of the drama, one can with better perspectives proceed to the intrinsic examination of it. The whole is, to be sure, a complicated web of interrelations and associations that can hardly be traced in full from the widely ranging interests of a lifetime. The main elements, however, stand out with some clarity, and it is helpful that Goethe himself pointed out the focus of creative synthesis in the passage in Plutarch that tells of "mothers as goddesses."[21] This passage, in the life of Marcellus, has long been known and regularly cited, but only as a bare passage, out of context, as though it were a source that Goethe employed instead of what it actually was for him: the point of synthesis, the catalyst, in a complex creative act. For right understanding, here as always, text must be seen within context. Only when it is, will its true importance and central position become manifest, making it clear why the passage meant to Goethe what it did, why it led to the results it did.

The immediate context at once assumes significance and enriches the fabric of connotation. Just before the passage on the Mothers Plutarch discourses at some length on the theme of the pure Platonic ideas, the lawful world of the intellect, as manifest in the abstract geometrical researches of Archimedes—all this in contrast first to the practical war machines he had devised at the request of King Hiero of Syracuse, and also in contrast to the senseless accident of his death when the city finally fell to the Romans, just as he was deep in thought on a difficult mathematical problem. Immediately after the passage on the Mothers, Plutarch relates that Marcellus was the first to bring great works of Greek art to Rome and to bring beauty, grace, and symmetry to a city which till then had been decorated only with the barbarous arms and spoils of war. To summarize in one image: the forms of Helen and Paris were brought into the Hall of the Knights. Incidentally, Marcellus also had some of the statues and pictures from Syracuse set up in Samothrace in the temple of the gods named Cabeiri.

The important point is that in Plutarch also the realm of the Mothers, on the one hand, has behind it the pure region of forms and ideas and, on the other hand, has issuing forth from it the exemplar of beauty into a barbarous martial culture.

But the passage on the Mothers itself also calls for closer scrutiny. The story of Nikias and the Mothers of Engyon is told at this point as an instance of the new gentleness and humanity that Marcellus was introducing into Roman affairs. The temple of the Mothers at Engyon is described as a very ancient one, built by the Cretans, presumably then of massive primordial construction, as was the one that in *Faust* magically appears on the stage in the Hall of the Knights. Among the votive gifts within the temple were the spears and bronze helmets of two of the heroes before Troy, both in earlier times suitors of Helen: storm-tossed Meriones and far-wandering Ulysses. Plutarch's story itself is concerned with Nikias, friend of the Romans, who, to escape the dominant Carthaginian faction in Engyon, at first feigned impiety toward the Mothers and then, on a carefully chosen public occasion, in the midst of an address, pretended to be stricken with madness by the goddesses and to flee in insane terror—out through the gates to freedom. He later interceded with Marcellus to save the city and let his enemies go free.

It seems to have remained unknown to Goethe scholarship that the poet, in all probability, read another, fuller account of the Mothers of Engyon. Just how well Goethe knew the world history of Diodorus Siculus in earlier years, is not known. He did borrow the German translation from the Weimar library on December 5, 1812, returning it on the following January 15.[22] Thus he probably read the section concerned with the Mothers at least this one time. According to Diodorus, the Mothers were goddesses from Crete; they were sometimes equated with the Idaean divinities who nursed Zeus safely through his infancy, while the Corybantes (Curetes, Cabeiri) with their noise helped the Great Mother, Rhea (Cybele), conceal her son from all-devouring Cronos. Here then is the motif of the successful defiance of Time by the nursing mother goddesses and the Great Mother.

Cretan Rhea was usually equated with Phrygian Cybele and often with the great mother of the fruitful earth, Demeter, not to mention the other mother and earth goddesses. This line of association has often been noted in connection with the scene in *Faust* and even the many-breasted Diana of the Ephesians was not forgotten. However, this association is afflicted by a fatal flaw: in each case, in each town and temple, there was only one Magna Mater, nowhere apparently except in Engyon and a few associated towns was there a group of mother goddesses. And yet there were two conspicuous as well as various minor exceptions. For one, Demeter was often or usually associated with her daughter, Sicilian Persephone, who in her various aspects was queen of the world of the dead, goddess of spring and new life, the virgin Kore, and also, according to one ancient tradition, the mother of Dionysus. Furthermore, Persephone preserved the images of all that once was, and we have already had a first glimpse of how closely she was associated in Goethe's mind with the whole complex of the Mother realm. Around the two goddesses, Demeter and Persephone, arose the mysteries of Eleusis, these in their turn were associated by several ancient writers with the mysteries of the Cabeiri of Samothrace and, by way of their common institutor, Orpheus, with the Dionysian mysteries, and also with the Delphic rites. More on this later in connection with Goethe's reading in Pausanias.

It is part of this whole complex of intertwining mythological associations that, according to one account (Pherecydes), Iasion was one of the Cabeiri. The standard accounts make Iasion the husband of Demeter and make Plutus, god of wealth, their son. It should be noted, therefore, that when Faust assumed the role of Plutus in the preceding carnival masque, he was relating himself closely to Persephone, the daughter of Demeter.

Of importance at this point is the fact that Persephone plays an important role in *Faust*, albeit behind the scenes: in the "Classical Walpurgis Night," Manto takes Faust down to the realm of Persephone, as she had earlier taken Orpheus, whereas the spectator goes on to the great genetic rites along the shores of the Aegean. We know that Goethe long intended to carry out the scene of Faust before Persephone, where he (or Manto) with a moving plea was to win Helena back to light and life. In the end Goethe did not carry out this scene but only suggested it symbolically by the course of events along the Aegean shore, the "stirb und werde" of ever renewed life. He could not have both the Mothers scene and the Persephone scene in the drama. He therefore chose the one that had the farthest symbolic reach and then suggested the other through a ritual pageant which, as I have previously shown, forms so beautiful a transition to the fifth as well as to the third act.[23]

But why could he not have both? The Persephone scene could have been one of the most moving in the whole of *Faust* and added further riches to a rich drama. The barriers to having both are considerations of form and tradition. On the formal side a Persephone scene would have been anticlimactic after a Mothers scene; the two would have weakened each other since both were concerned with essentially the same theme: the hero venturing beyond the normal bounds of place and time to gain something of high importance. That brings up a pervasive tradition that has never been observed in its relation to *Faust*, even though Goethe pointed to it in the words of Manto (7493) and clearly wanted the reader to make the association that brings Faust into symbolic relation to the legendary hero (here Orpheus) and his perilous venture.

From prehistoric hero tales on through Renaissance epic tradition, the hero, at the height of his venturesome undertakings, embarks upon a perilous voyage beyond the known world, and usually returns with added power or treasure, tangible or intangible, though occasionally tragedy intervenes. Such a venture often stands as a symbol of the hero's acceptance as a hero by the higher powers (I use the word "hero" in its ancient sense). It is adumbrated in the eleventh book of the *Odyssey*, it is fully developed in the sixth book of the *Aeneid* (where Aeneas himself cites the precedents), it is all-comprising in the *Argonauts* and in a very different way in the *Divine Comedy* (notable here also the strange tale of the voyage of Ulysses to the antipodes), and it is infinitely varied in the Renaissance epic.

As a pass and safeguard on the venture Aeneas takes with him the golden bough. The two heroes of *Jerusalem Delivered* who make the perilous voyage to the Fortunate Isles and the magic garden of Armida to rescue Rinaldo, are equipped by the Christian magus with a golden wand to fend off all perils. Faust is equipped with a gleaming, warding key, a Janus symbol, necessary here for reasons that will be explained later. The fourteenth book of the *Jerusalem Delivered*, with its description of the gorgeous palace of the magus down in the enchanted depths is also in other ways of singular importance in the study of Goethe's imagery and motifs. Curious how this relationship has been neglected despite the poet's affectionate remembrance of the work as a favorite of his younger years. For our present purposes it is important in calling attention to another associated tradition, stemming from Vergil's fourth *Georgic* and continuing to Sannazaro's *Arcadia* and beyond.

One can observe the associations to various scenes in the second part of *Faust* as Vergil unfolds the tale of Aristaeus the shepherd who is afflicted by a strange curse and implores his mother, the nymph Cyrene, to give him aid.[24] In their palace beneath the depths, the nymphs are spinning and listening to the tale of the countless loves of the gods from Chaos on. The waters are parted asunder and Aristaeus descends into the depths. "And now, marvelling at his mother's home, a realm of waters, at the lakes locked in caverns, and the echoing groves, he went on his way, and dazed by the mighty rush of waters, he gazed on all the rivers, as, each in his own place, they glide under the great earth." On his mother's advice they go for counsel to wise old Proteus. "To him we Nymphs do reverence, and aged Nereus himself; for the seer has knowledge of all things—what is, what hath been, what is in train ere long to happen." Through his mother's stratagem the son makes Proteus stay and give answer (one is reminded of the earlier account of Menelaos in the fourth book of the *Odyssey*). Aristaeus learns that the curse upon him was invoked by Orpheus because he had frightened Eurydice into the flight that led to her death from the serpent's sting. There follows the account of Orpheus' entrance into the underworld, the phantoms gathering around him enchanted by his song, his winning of Eurydice and losing her again, her sad farewell that anticipates Helena's farewell to Faust: "Lo, again the cruel Fates call me back and sleep veils my swimming eyes. And now farewell! I am swept off, wrapped in uttermost night, and stretching out to thee strengthless hands, thine, alas! no more." With the same creative proteanism with which Vergil formed and transformed these ancient poetic motifs, Goethe allows them to echo and re-echo in the Mothers scene, in the "Classical Walpurgis Night," and in the Helena act.

Perhaps closest of all to Goethe's Mother realm, the realm itself rather than the Mothers as such, are features of the region of the moon as Ariosto describes them in cantos thirty-four and thirty-five of his *Orlando Furioso* on Astolfo's voyage thither. In one valley there is stored and preserved what was lost on earth. Then Astolfo sees how at the hands of the Fates things present enter into the realm of the past, usually going down to oblivion, in rare instances being rescued and preserved in the Temple of Fame. He also visits the hall of the future, and finally learns that all in this realm is in symbolic or schematic relation to what is and happens on earth. "You should know that not a leaf moves down there that does not give here a sign of itself. It is necessary that every event should correspond on earth and in Heaven, but with a different face."[25] It would be more interesting than profitable to trace the tradition on to Marino's *Adone*, Book Ten, and Camoëns' *Lusiads*, Book Nine. Suffice it to note that in the one there is a remarkable fusion of the Ariosto and the Claudianus traditions, and in the other the same correspondence as in Ariosto between the realities and the schemata. This is, of course, a reversal of the Platonic concept of the archetypes; for these poets the archetypes are not the ultimate realities but only the schemata, for them the earthly phenomena are not mere shadows or reflections of a higher reality, they are reality itself. Goethe, here and elsewhere, is in accord with this anti-Platonic tradition. Critics have, of course, noticed the presence of Platonic elements in this scene but have not noticed that the poet has reversed them in the manner of his literary predecessors. Again the danger of a merely philosophical intellectual approach becomes obvious when the result is a confusion of even the thought content and the basic premises.

Though the realm of the Mothers, once it had taken form and place in the drama, supplanted the Persephone scene, it also assimilated the symbolic and connotative values of the Persephone-Demeter complex, as a glance at the Faustian text will show (6212 ff.). There is the element of the mysteries and initiation, with mystagogue and neophyte (in this instance a cynical yet exceptionally sincere and earnest mystagogue and an at first suspicious yet venturesome and then committed neophyte), with a course of initiation which, as in all the great mysteries, must first make real to the initiate the meaning of death, total extinction, utter loneliness, and then lead him on, through deep ineffable terror, to the mystic glowing hearth of rebirth, of constantly renewed life, of the awareness of his oneness with the totality of life. Locked door and proferred key have ever been accompanying symbols of the mysteries.

Added to this is the mysterious nature of the two goddesses, their perplexing ambiguity (not in the school mythologies, to be sure, but in the actualities of Greek myth and worship). In the case of the mother that is well illustrated in the Homeric hymn to Demeter, particularly in the tale of her coming to Eleusis and the home of Celeus, from which Goethe carried over motifs into the Helena act, redoubling their ambiguity. It is not unintentional on Goethe's part that Demeter's mask here of ancient housekeeper from Crete should go over strangely transformed into the Helena act:

> ... in fashion she was like an ancient crone. ... Such are the housekeepers in their echoing halls. ...

> ... from Crete am I come hither over the wide ridges of the sea, by no will of my own, nay, by violence have sea-rovers brought me hither under duress. ...

> ... the Goddess stood on the threshold, her head touching the roof-beam, and she filled the doorway with the light divine.

> Then wonder, and awe, and pale fear seized the mother. ...

Near the end of the poem come the words on the establishing of the Eleusinian mysteries:

> ... she showed them the manner of her rites, and taught them her goodly mysteries, holy mysteries which none may violate, or search into, or noise abroad, for the great curse from the Gods restrains the voice. Happy is he among deathly men who hath beheld these things! and he that is uninitiate, and hath no lot in them, hath never equal lot in death beneath the murky gloom.[26]

In the case of the daughter, I have already suggested her indeterminacy. Goethe developed it in a poem that, with title and subtitle, is worth quoting here (W.A. I, 3:130):

KORE
Nicht gedeutet!

Ob Mutter? Tochter? Schwester? Enkelin?
Von Helios gezeugt? Von wer geboren?
Wohin gewandert? Wo versteckt? Verloren?
Gefunden?—Rätsel ists dem Künstlersinn.
Und ruhte sie verhüllt in düstre Schleier,
Vom Rauch umwirbelt acherontischer Feuer,
Die Gott-Natur enthüllt sich zum Gewinn:
Nach höchster Schönheit muß die Jungfrau streben,
Sizilien verleiht ihr Götterleben.

KORE
Not interpreted

Or mother? daughter? sister? daughter's child?
Begot by Helios? brought forth by whom?
Whereunto wandered? Hidden where? What doom?
Recovered?—Riddle to the artist's mind.
And though she rest enwrapped in drear attire
Enswirled by smoke of Acherontic fire,
Her godly nature shines forth undefiled.
Toward highest beauty must the maiden strive,
Sicilia dowers her with godly life.

The mystery underlying the Eleusinian rites is the perennial mystery of the cycle of life in birth and death and rebirth, as it is symbolized yearly in the cycle of the seasons. The lesser mysteries (at Agrae) centered upon the joyful wonder of birth, the new life of nascent spring, with Kore returning from the realm of the dead. The greater Eleusinian mysteries, celebrated in the autumn, centered upon the tragic wonder of the fruition that is also the portal of death. Here, as a central feature of the rites, a case or chest was opened and its contents taken up or touched by the worshipers. The secret of what was in the case died with antiquity and its religion; great has been the speculation since about it. It is unnecessary to take seriously the most recent guesses which generally tend in a Victorian-Freudian direction. If we keep in mind the two main factors of which we do have firm knowledge, the simple and beautiful answer to the enigma will come without effort. It is well documented that the worshipers came from the initiatory rites consoled, uplifted, and with a new confidence in life. Demeter was a grain goddess, a goddess of the fruitful earth; Persephone was goddess of death, in the underworld during the barren third of the year, and returned to earth each year as the goddess of springtime and flowers. The sacred chest is a symbolic tomb. If in the gloom of autumn its contents could bring ultimate revelation and consolation to the worshipers, what could it have contained? Probably, almost certainly: sprouted grains of wheat, the symbol of dying and becoming, the grain buried and perishing in the autumn, yet in death sending forth the green shoots of winter wheat that promised an abundant harvest for the following year.

This central Eleusinian mystery of death and resurrection is also symbolically the central mystery of the Mothers scene, as the next chapter will show. More than that, it is the central mystery of the whole Faust drama, set forth most clearly in four places, namely, near the beginning and end of each part. Near the close of Faust's first great scene his imminent death by suicide is countered by the Easter chorus singing "Christ is arisen." In the concluding prison scene Mephistopheles' verdict on Gretchen, "She is judged," is countered by the voice from above, "She is saved." At the beginning of the second part Faust, in total collapse after the catastrophe, is in the symbolic passage of time restored by the benign spirits of nature whom Ariel exhorts: "From suffered horror cleanse his inner self" (4625), "Restore him to the holy light" (4633). Near the end of the second part, after Faust's death, Mephistopheles again renders his verdict, "The last, poor, empty moment" (11589), and is again countered by the verdict from on high:

> Gerettet ist das edle Glied   11934
> Der Geisterwelt vom Bösen.

The noble branch of the spirit world   11934
Is rescued now from evil.

Formation, transformation is at the heart of the life process and its continuing cycle. It is also at the heart of the Mothers scene and at the heart of Goethe's own thinking, poetic and scientific. It is necessary to look more closely at this central formulation of his morphological perception.

As in the enigma of the poem on Kore, so in the mystery of the mother goddesses: when it comes to the main point of their function and divinity, the indeterminacy resolves into clarity and beauty of purpose. So also in the *Faust:* immediately after the words suggesting their strange indeterminacy (which have an aesthetic intent, as will appear) come the clear and unmistakable words on their function:

> *Some sit, some stand, some wander to and fro,*   6286
> *As it may chance. Formation, transformation,*
> *Eternal mind's eternal recreation.*

"Gestaltung, Umgestaltung," "formation, transformation," are key words in Goethe, both in his poetry and in his science. It is clear from the text itself what he means here, but in order that no doubt remain (particularly in view of the interpretations that neglect this functional description and its dynamic, creative implications), we should note how he uses them elsewhere in context. Of the various instances that could be cited, a few characteristic ones will suffice, drawn from his scientific writings on morphology, from an even earlier aesthetic essay, and from his poetry.

    The introduction he wrote for his morphological studies in 1807 bears the title "Bildung und Umbildung organischer Naturen," "Shaping and Re-shaping of Organic Beings." In it he observes that the word "Gestalt," "form," in usage is deprived of its quality of movement and made fixed and rigid. Thus, it should either not be used in the field of morphology or, if it is used, we should think of it as something that in experience is held firm only for the moment. He himself goes on to use derivatives of "bilden":

> *The shaped is at once reshaped again, and we, if we wish to attain*
> *to a passably vivid view of nature, must keep ourselves just as mobile*
> *and pliant, in accordance with the example she offers us.*[27]

Even earlier, in 1798, he had used this formulation. The fact that he had done so in connection with his art studies is important. In his preliminary outlines for the essays on art criticism in the *Propyläen*, there are the following entries under the general heading "I. Von der Natur zur Kunst," "From nature to art":

> *Where the scientist apprehends the beginnings of forms.—Final results of organization.—Realization through shaping and reshaping.—On to the human form in general.*[28]

In his monograph of 1820 on the intermaxillary bone (which begins with his little treatise of 1784, at the time of discovery) he has ventured on to using "Gestalt" dynamically:

> *With so much having been said about formation and transformation, the question arises whether one can really derive the skull bones from the vertebrae, whether one should and may still recognize their original form despite such great and decisive changes.*[29]

He goes on, in a highly significant passage, to develop his principle of indeterminacy in the sciences.

In his periodical, *Zur Naturwissenschaft überhaupt, besonders zur Morphologie*, he printed the following poem, later entitled "Parabase":

> Freudig war vor vielen Jahren
> Eifrig so der Geist bestrebt,
> Zu erforschen, zu erfahren,
> Wie Natur im Schaffen lebt.
> Und es ist das ewig Eine,
> Das sich vielfach offenbart:
> Klein das Große, groß das Kleine
> Alles nach der eignen Art;
> Immer wechselnd, fest sich haltend,
> Nah und fern und fern und nah,
> So gestaltend, umgestaltend—
> Zum Erstaunen bin ich da.

> *Joyfully in years gone by*
> *Eager did the spirit strive*
> *To explore and to experience*
> *Creative nature here alive.*
> *And it is eternal oneness*

Manifoldly here enshrined:
Small the great and great the small one
Wholly after its own kind;
Always changing, holding firmly,
Near and far and far and near,
Thus with forming and transforming—
For amazement I am here.[30]

Here are both the "formation, transformation" and, in paraphrase, the "eternal mind's eternal recreation."

In his poem on the metamorphosis of animals he uses the felicitous summary designation, "bewegliche Ordnung," "movable order." In his poem "Eins und Alles" of 1821 the phrasing is varied again, quite in consonance with the subject, in the third stanza (W.A. I, 3, 81):

Und umzuschaffen das Geschaffne,
Damit sichs nicht zum Starren waffne,
Wirkt ewiges, lebendges Tun.

To recreate the once created,
Prevent its growing indurated,
Requires eternal living act.

and in the fourth, concluding:

Es soll sich regen, schaffend handeln,
Erst sich gestalten, dann verwandeln;
Nur scheinbar stehts Momente still.
Das Ewge regt sich fort in allen;
Denn alles muß in Nichts zerfallen,
Wenn es im Sein beharren will.

It should, creatively alert,
First move to form and then convert;
Only for moments it seems still.
The eternal moves in all that's wrought;
For everything must fall to naught
If in mere being lies its will.

Here again, a paraphrase of the "eternal mind's eternal recreation" in a line that Goethe repeats as the second line of a poem written in answer and supplement to this one (W.A. I, 3:82):

Kein Wesen kann zu nichts zerfallen,
Das Ewge regt sich fort in allen.

No being can fall into naught,
The eternal moves in all that's wrought.

This morphological principle of "formation, transformation" had already been associated with the *Faust* itself, specifically the Helena act, before the Mothers scene was written, as two letters will demonstrate. To Sulpiz Boisserée Goethe wrote October 22, 1826:

The Helena is one of my oldest conceptions, contemporaneous with the Faust, *always with the same intent, always shaped and reshaped.*

And to Nees von Esenbeck, May 25, 1827:

In how manifold a way has this [Helena] been formed and transformed through long, scarcely measurable years.[31]

Goethe's careful and purposeful introduction of the functional concept of "formation, transformation" into the realm of the Mothers, followed immediately by the concept of the eternal maintenance of the eternal intent, "Des ewigen Sinnes ewige Unterhaltung," "Eternal mind's eternal recreation," indicates that here too, in the disembodied realm of images ("Bilder," "Schemen"), the all-pervasive universal laws of dynamic metamorphosis prevail. What happens here in the immaterial ("Around them is no place, still less a time," "Into the unbound realm of forms," "They do not see you, forms alone they see") is a true counterpart of what happens in the concrete, where place and time prevail, in the finite realm of the created, where *logos* becomes *anthropos*. If one should feel tempted to think of this realm as a mere dead, vague, purposeless realm of the past, one need only to call to mind the highly dynamic explosion that occurs when Faust wilfully tries to interfere with its lawful course.

There is clearly a symbolic intent in the poet's having the Helena action begin and end with a process of "formation, transformation." In the "Hall of the Knights" her form first emerges as the incense cloud that arises from the tripod, shapes, reshapes, and assumes form. At the beginning of the fourth act her garments, which had turned into clouds and carried Faust back to the mountains of the north, float off into the distance, at first retaining the majestic form of divine womanhood—Juno, Leda, Helena—and then becoming formless, towering cloud, like distant icy mountains brilliantly reflecting the fleeting days' great meaning.

With all this, one negating factor has been lurking in the background, threatening to upset and nullify the entire carefully searching process. For it remains an undeniable feature of the whole that the description of the realm of the Mothers in the scene "Dark Gallery" comes from Mephistopheles, who can tell the truth when he has to or when he chooses to (for instance, in order to becloud a situation still more), but who cannot be relied on to do so. Even here, where he does tell the truth as a last resort, because there is no other way out (he must fulfill Faust's request, he cannot do so by his own powers), he manages to give it a negative twist and to make Faust object: "For in your naught I hope to find the all" (6256).

Though Faust's initial suspicion and rejection give way to acceptance once he holds the key in hand and feels its power, though he becomes convinced that Mephistopheles, this once at least, is telling the truth, the critic has every reason to suspend belief and allow for the possibility of a trickery even more subtle than heretofore until he is convinced on evidence from a more reliable witness.

The more reliable witness is Faust himself when he returns from the realm of the Mothers and reports what he has experienced. His words (6427–38) carry as much the conviction of truth as of poetic grandeur, and there is not the slightest indication anywhere in the text that Mephistopheles in the prompter's box controls them as he does the words of the astrologer. Quite the opposite: when he does try to influence the course of Faust's words and actions (6501 *et seq.*), he clearly shows himself unable to do so. The critical hypothesis that Faust is in conspiracy with Mephistopheles to deceive the Emperor and his court is also contrary to text. Every word and act of Faust is that of a man completely uncalculating and unaware of any audience or any ulterior purpose. Word and act lead, in fact, to the defeat of any such alleged Mephistophelean intent as Faust impetuously brings the scene to its calamitous end.

What does Faust tell us about the realm of the Mothers, after he has been there? It is in the boundless, the eternally lonely. The goddesses themselves dwell in companionship. The images of life hover about them, moving, lifeless. That which once was, in the realm of appearances, continues moving, has the will to last forever. The goddesses, all powerful, distribute it to the realm of day and night (that includes, of course, back to the world of time, to the future, as the next lines show). Some of the images are seized and taken up into life's lovely course, others are sought out by the confident magus who is able to make manifest the wondrous. In this setting "magus" probably means the creative master of forms, the artist poet. The realm of forms and images is the one the artist has at his command. In an earlier draft Goethe actually wrote "Dichter," "poet," instead of "magus."

Though this account differs from that of Mephistopheles in point of view and accent, it agrees with it on the whole and does not contradict it at any point. Mephistopheles had warned (6291) that the danger was great, and on Faust's disappearance speculated whimsically on whether he would ever return. Faust also refers to his venture as "Mein Schreckensgang," "my fearful journey" (6489).

If further demonstration is required for the intrinsic validity of this scene, there is an abundance of evidence coming from three different directions: the larger context of the drama as a whole, the more sensitive regard for poetic tone and level of diction, and (most decisively) Goethe's own plans, sketches, remarks, and reflections.

As for the larger context, the third chapter has already examined one dramatic continuum in which this scene has an important place. All the other contextual relationships that emerge in the course of this study lead to the same conclusion: in full context only the interpretation of serious intent is possible and the other interpretations are excluded as discrepant and out of harmony with the whole.

With regard to the poetic tone and level of diction, a discriminating ear will detect distinct differences in the various speeches of Mephistopheles that are concerned with the theme of creativity. In those passages where Mephistopheles, the anti-creative, is free to ridicule creative matters, he does so, often obviously, sometimes more subtly, but always with the wittily vicious word choice and higher voice level appropriate to the occasion. Quite different, however, is the choice of seriously appropriate words and the lower, less strident voice level in those passages where, quite against his will and nature, he must, in accordance with his wager, fulfill Faust's request, even when this involves him in a statement about creative phenomena basically contrary to his negative destructive impulses. This is the case with Mephistopheles' description of the realm of the Mothers. Those few critics who have approached the drama

primarily from the artistic, poetic, mythic side have confidently come to like
conclusions about the credibility and sincerity of Mephistopheles in this and
comparable passages; thus Karl Kerényi in his investigations of Goethe's mythic
imagination, and Kurt May in his examination of the formal aspects of speech
and sound, diction and expression.[32]

Goethe's several synopses of the action indicate plainly the kind of role
he intended Mephistopheles to play in the recovery of Helen, a role far from
masterful. Simultaneously, the poet's intent with regard to Helen and her return
comes distinctly to view and negates deviant interpretations that have won
some favor. From the beginning a double appearance for Helen is planned:
the Helen that Faust first sees is to be an intangible form that cannot be held;
but the Helen that Faust finally wins is, within the understanding of the drama,
to be the real Helen, not a specter or dream vision. In his synopsis of 1816
the accompanying circumstances are quite different but the central conditions
are already established:

> Helen belongs to Orcus, and though she can be enticed forth through
> magic arts, she cannot be retained. . . .
> [Later] Helen appears; through a magic ring corporeality is restored
> to her.[33]

This differentiation also occurs in the synopsis of December, 1826, here somewhat closer to final form and, significantly, accompanied by a clear statement
on Mephistopheles' disability in the classical world:

> During a great festival at the German emperor's court . . .Faust and
> Mephistopheles . . . summon up the desired likenesses (phantoms)
> of Helen and Paris. . . .
> [Later] Faust, called back into life from a deep long somnolence,
> during which his dreams transpire visibly in detail before the eyes of
> the spectator, steps forth exalted and, completely imbued with this
> most sublime vision, urgently demands possession of her from
> Mephistopheles. The latter, who does not like to admit that he has
> no authority in the classical Hades, is not even welcome there, makes
> use of his old tested means of distracting his superior to and fro in
> all directions . . . [and so on, to the employment of Homunculus].[34]

Thus Goethe's intent is clear, not only here, but also in the final text,
when carefully read. In the first place, Faust is not in a dream state when he

goes on his quest for Helen (he is clearly made to awaken when he touches Greek soil near the beginning of the "Classical Walpurgis Night"). Furthermore, the Helen of his first vision in the "Hall of the Knights" is an *eidolon*, a likeness, an apparition, an image, but the Helen he finally wins back to light and life is, within the sense and circumstance of the drama, the real Helen, however imperiled her hold on the new life. And finally, Mephistopheles is "out of his element," of himself unable to help Faust, at first reluctant to admit his impotence, and then of necessity seeking other, more effective instrumentalities for accomplishing Faust's request.

CHAPTER NINE: PAUSANIAS AND PROTEAN MYTH

Another such journey as Faust's, for a great prize equally intangible, with an equally alarming after-effect, is to be found in the same complex of Orphic, Delphic mystery and divination in which the rest of the Mothers myth is embedded. I refer specifically to the descent to the oracle of Trophonius, which the quester had to undertake alone, amid terrors from which he only gradually recovered. Pausanias' description of Greece, which Goethe consulted at various times over the course of four decades, particularly for his art studies, has the most extensive account of this oracle. Here it is in the English translation of Thomas Taylor (1794) which Goethe himself used in 1827:

> *When anyone desires to descend into the cave of Trophonius, he must first take up residence for a certain number of days in a building destined to this purpose. This building is a temple of the Good Daemon, and of Good Fortune. While he stays here he purifies himself . . . he . . . sacrifices to Trophonius and his sons; to Apollo, Saturn, and Jupiter the King; to Juno the chariot driver, and to Ceres, whom they call Europa, and who they say was the nurse of Trophonius. . . . He is . . . brought to the fountains of the river . . . [and] obliged to drink of that which is called the water of Lethe, that he may become oblivious of all the former objects of his pursuit. Afterwards he must drink of another water, which is called the water of Mnemosyne, or memory, that he may remember the objects which will present themselves to his view on descending into the [cave]. Having therefore beheld the statue, which they say was made by Daedalus (and which the priests never shew to any but those who desire to consult Trophonius), performed certain religious ceremonies, and prayed, he proceeds to the oracle clothed in white linen, begirt with fillets, and having on his feet such slippers as are worn by the natives of this place. The oracle is above the grove in a mountain, and is inclosed with a wall of white stone, whose circumference is*

*very small, and whose altitude is not more than two cubits. Two
obelisks are raised on this wall, which, as well as the zones that hold
them together, are of brass. Between these there are doors: and
within the inclosure there is a chasm of the earth, which was not
formed by nature, but was made by art, and is excavated in according
proportion with consummate accuracy and skill. The shape of this
chasm resembles that of an oven. . . . There are not steps to its
bottom: but when any one designs to descend to Trophonius, they
give him a ladder, which is both narrow and light. On descending
into this chasm, between its bottom and summit there is a small
cavern, the breadth of which is about two spans, and its altitude
appears to be about one span.*

*He, therefore, who descends to the bottom of this chasm lays himself
down on the ground, and holding in his hand sops mingled with
honey, first of all places his feet in the small cavern, then hastens to
join his knees to his feet; and immediately after the rest of his body
contracted to his knees, is drawn within the cavern, just as if he was
hurried away by the vortex of the largest and most rapid river. But
those that have descended to the adytum of this place are not all
instructed in the secrets of futurity in the same manner. For one
obtains this knowledge by his sight, and another by his hearing: but
all return through the same opening, and walk backward as they
return. . . . When the person that descended to Trophonius returns,
the sacrificers immediately place him on a throne, which they call
the throne of Mnemosyne, and which stands not far from the adytum.
Then they ask him what he has either seen or heard, and afterwards
deliver him to certain persons appointed for this purpose, who bring
him to the temple of Good Fortune, and the Good Daemon, while
he is yet full of terror, and without any knowledge either of himself,
or of those that are near him. Afterwards, however, he recovers the
use of his reason, and laughs just the same as before. . . .*[35]

This last, with the added statement of personal direct knowledge,
Pausanias no doubt set down in order to refute rumors (and a proverbial
saying) circulating in the ancient world that no one who entered the cave of
Trophonius ever smiled again. Plutarch ("Sulla," XVII) records that two who
had gone down to Trophonius agreed in this, that they had seen one who in
beauty and majesty was similar to Jupiter Olympus—the way Goethe later

came to visualize the Earth Spirit as he appeared to Faust. Plutarch's strange
tale of what Timarchus saw in the cave of Trophonius ("Socrates' Daimon,"
XXI–XXII) also has varied affiliations to this whole complex of myth and
image. Not to be overlooked in Pausanias' account is the recurrent motif of
Lethe-Mnemosyne which is also basic in the *Faust* scene and will move to a
more central position in the considerations of the next chapter.

Pausanias is particularly rich in connotative passages that could have
added greatly to the depth and scope of Goethe's evolving myth of the Mothers
and other related image complexes in *Faust*. That any particular passage did so,
must remain uncertain since similar stimuli could and probably did come to him
from the wide variety of other ancient authors he read. But as characteristic
specimens of the kind of images that impinged upon his imagination and could
be assimilated into the *Faust* the following may serve:

> *And here [on the promontory of Colias] the statues of Venus Colias,*
> *and of the goddesses who are called Genetyllides, are contained. But*
> *it appears to me that these divinities . . . are the same with those*
> *goddesses which the Phocaeans, a people of Ionia, call Gennaides*
> *(Pausanias 1:5, p. 3 f.)*
> *Near to this is the temple of Ceres, in which the statue of the goddess*
> *herself, of her daughter Proserpine, and of Iacchus holding a torch,*
> *are contained (II:4, p. 5 f.)*

Here a passage on the defense of the shrine of Delphi against the Gauls, with
a remarkable parallel to the imperial battle of act four:

> *But as soon as the engagement began, it is reported that thunder fell*
> *upon the Gauls, and fragments of rock torn from Parnassus; and*
> *that three armed men of terrible appearance stood before the*
> *Barbarians. . . . The Pergamenians yet retain the spoils of the*
> *Gauls . . . the land which is inhabited by the Pergamenians is said*
> *to be sacred to the Cabiri (IV:4 and 6, p. 11 f.).*

After an account of Ceres, Proserpina, and Triptolemus:

> *It was my intention, indeed, to have related every particular about*
> *the temple at Athens, which is called Eleusinian, but I was restrained*
> *from the execution of this design by a vision in a dream. I shall,*
> *therefore, return to such particulars as it is lawful to disclose (XIV:3,*
> *p. 39 f.).*

But an epigram in this place signifies that Celestial Venus is the eldest of those divinities who are called the Parcae (XIX:2, p. 51).

There is also a temple of Earth the nurse of youths, and of virid Ceres. But the reason of these appellations may be known from the priests (XXII:3, p. 61).

But Aeschylus was the first that represented these divinities [the Erinnys] with snakes in their hair; for neither the statues of these goddesses, nor any other of the subterranean divinities, are in the least dreadful in their appearance (XXVIII:6, p. 82).

But another temple contains the altars of Ceres Anesidora, of Ctesian Jupiter, of Minerva Tithrone, of first-born Proserpine, and of the goddesses which they call Severe (XXXI:4, p. 93).

The Greeks report, that Nemesis was the mother of Helen, but that Leda was her nurse. . . . Phidias . . . represented Helen led by Leda to Nemesis (XXXIII:7–8, p. 100).

But he that has been initiated in the Eleusinian mysteries, or has read the poems called Orphic, will know what I mean. (XXXVII:4, p. 109).

But the Pythian deity would not suffer Coroebus to return to Argos, but ordered him to carry a tripod from the temple, and that in whatever place the tripod should fall, he should there build a temple to Apollo, and there fix his habitation (XLIII:8, p. 128).

Let these specimens, from only the first book out of ten, suffice to indicate the plenitude of visions, the "Fülle der Gesichte," that flitted past the window of Goethe's imagination as he read Pausanias. Sources? by no means; in-fluences perhaps, in the sense of images assimilated into a greater whole. What is important, though, is the general and total impression of the endless proteanism of it all, the "formation, transformation," the manifold aspects, under and through all of which, nevertheless, runs the worshipful reverence for the all-encompassing power of life going through its endless cycles of birth and death and birth again, the feminine principle of nature, clear in its ultimate meaning, yet ever mysterious and unfathomable in its processes.

This is the underlying ground of so much of the indefinable surrounding the realm of the Mothers in *Faust* and the closely related parts of the "Classical Walpurgis Night" and the Helena act. It is an integral part of these scenes and actions, without which they would not achieve poetic truth; it can never be wholly explained, never be explained away. That is perhaps why Goethe refused to discuss the matter with Eckermann (January 10, 1830):

He, however, in his usual manner enveloped himself in mystery,
looking at me wide-eyed and repeating the words: "The
Mothers! Mothers! it sounds so strangely weird!"[36]

All that another can do is to observe how in Goethe's poetic development, in
the *Faust* and outside it, the concept of the feminine, maternal principle, in all
its mystery, developed with ever richer and deeper connotations until he
finally found the ultimate magic-poetic formula which could penetrate to the
vital center and offer the definitive poetic statement of the mystery.

There is one further element of major importance that entered into this creative complex and indeed gave all this morphological, cyclic-generative indeterminacy the necessary contour and form for poetic presentation. These firm contours and noble forms probably entered into Goethe's creative vision from ancient sculpture, for one, from a work of Hellenistic art, "The Apotheosis of Homer," a bas-relief by Archelaos of Priene (*ca.* 125 B.C.). Goethe had seen the original work itself at the Colonna Palace in Rome and had it well in mind when years later he wrote an interpretative essay on it. By this time, in 1827, the bas-relief was already in the British Museum. Casts of four separate figures from it had just reached him in late September, and he at once borrowed from the library the standard older treatise on the subject, Gisbert Cuperus' *Apotheosis vel Consecratio Homeri* (Amsterdam: 1683), which contained the large folded engraving of the relief by Giovanni Battista Galestruzzi (Galostruccius) of 1658 and further engravings of associated works. So absorbed was he by this study, especially by one enigma for which he found the explanation, namely the man and tripod at the right, that only a few days later, on October 3, 1827, he wrote the preliminary sketch of his essay, "Homers Apotheose."

As chance or fate would have it, this happened at just the time when he was writing the scenes in the first act of the second part of *Faust* that immediately precede those of the Mothers. Moreover at just this time he was receiving the critical and personal reactions to the recently published Helena act—with the kind of interest that can be observed especially well in his important letter to Iken of the previous week (September 23). The essay itself contains such hints and anticipations of the crucial connecting scene of the Mothers (still to be written, two and a quarter years later) that the subconscious continuity emerges before the observing eye. Let us first look at excerpts from Goethe's description:

> *Clearly discernable . . . is the divine homage to Homer depicted on the lower part of the relief. . . .*

> *On the mountain height Zeus sitting. . . . Mnemosyne has just*

*received from him the permission for the deification of her favorite . . .
she the mother of all poetry. . . .*

*A younger muse, springing down with childlike gaiety, makes joyful
announcement to her seven sisters who, sitting and standing on the
middle plain, seem to be attending to that which transpired above.
Then one perceives a cave, there Apollo Musagetes in the traditional
long singer's robe. . . .*

*From above, then, the divine patent is conferred and proclaimed to
the two middle rows. The lowest, fourth plane, however, . . . represents
the real, albeit poetic-symbolic conferring of the granted high honor.*

*What remains problematic, however, are two more figures in the
right niche of the second row from below. On a pedestal stands the
figure of a man of middle years. . . . In his right hand he holds a
paper or vellum roll and over his head can be seen the upper part
of a tripod. . . .*[37]

Then follows Goethe's interpretation, which has remained the accepted
one: this represents a poet who had won a tripod through a poetic work,
probably in honor of Homer, and who appears here in a commemorative
tablet. In a preliminary sketch he also mentions the ninth muse, between the
poet and Apollo, presenting to the latter the roll that probably contained the
prize-winning poem. It is strange that the *Faust* critics have always interpreted
the tripod in the realm of the Mothers according to its Delphic prophetic
connotations and have never brought out its also prevalent ancient use as a
symbol of poetic achievement, even when they (rightly) interpret this scene as
symbolic of the poetic-creative process.

Whereas earlier results led to the more conceptual explication of the
central descriptive words on the realm of the Mothers—

> *Some sit, some stand, some wander to and fro,*   6286
> *As it may chance. Formation, transformation,*
> *Eternal mind's eternal recreation.*

—here is the sculptural embodiment of the words. The Muses are informally
arranged on the two planes, grouped sitting, standing, and striding, in seemingly
random sequence, and we have Goethe's descriptive words, "sitting and standing," "sitzend und stehend." That the poet had ancient sculptured figures in
mind (or rather "in image") for the first line cited can also be seen strikingly
in his remarks to Eckermann (April 1, 1827) :

[For an actor then] it is quite essential . . . that he has carefully studied
the works of sculpture that have come down to us and has carefully
absorbed the unaffected grace of their sitting, standing, and walking.[38]

Thus one vital descriptive line in the Mothers scene, "Die einen sitzen, andre
stehn und gehn" (6286), is, in context and connotation, firmly established as
coming from the aesthetic vocabulary of Goethe's art criticism: "sitzend und
stehend," "Sitzens, Stehens und Gehens." With all the casual informality,
"Wie's eben kommt," there is a firm order and sequence in this group on the
middle plane: the mother, Mnemosyne, establishes the connection upward to
the Olympian father; Clio, Muse of history, on the one hand, establishes the
relation from the commemorated poet to Apollo, and on the other hand leads
over to the group on the lower plane celebrating the ritual of the apotheosis of
Homer.

The realm of the Muses, then, in this bas-relief is a realm mediate between the decrees of heaven and the happenings on earth, with the poet-creator
also standing in a mediating position, backed up by the symbol of the *vates-*
poeta, the Delphic tripod. But the Muses as mother goddesses? Yes, by clear
implication in Greek mythology, and quite explicitly in Roman mythology. In
Greece they are by origin nymphs of spring and song, who through their connection with Apollo Musagetes possess the gift of prophecy, and altogether
represent the human effort to give permanence to the passing, "dem Augenblick
Dauer verleihen." It is in Rome, however, that one clearly finds the extension
of their attributes to those here most pertinent: the poets equated them with
the Camenae (Casmenae), prophetic nymphs of spring and goddesses of birth.

It is possible to go one step further, led by Goethe who here describes
Mnemosyne as the mother of all poetry. According to the usual mythological
accounts, the Muses are daughters of Zeus and Mnemosyne. Mnemosyne her-
self is in mythology one of the "Urmütter," the Titanides, the sister of Tethys,
Rhea, Themis, Phoebe, Dione, Thia, from whom the race of the classic Greek
gods sprang. Thus one could put the analogy tersely by stating that Faust's
perilous voyage led to the realm of memory. Memory is the mother of the
Muses. There is no art without recollection.

In the bas-relief, the *poïetēs*, the poet-creator, with the tripod behind
him, holds a manuscript roll in his right hand. What did Goethe mean by
equipping his counterpart, Faust, with a gleaming key for his entrance into the
realm of the Mothers? Within the bounds of Graeco-Roman mythology, which
to this point has proved adequate for the explication of the scene (with certain
Renaissance accretions, to be sure), the most obvious figure who bears the
attribute of the key is Janus, the god of the beginnings and origins of all

things, looking backward at the past and forward into the future, the guiding divinity of this whole scene, concerned as it is with the cycle of the revolving years, with new beginnings, with the continuity of past, through present, to future. One could go so far as to say that somehow, however unobtrusively, the Janus symbol had to be introduced into this scene of a perilous voyage across the boundaries of place and time; and so the key takes over the duty of the conventional sceptre, wand, or bough in the hand of the venturesome hero.

The reason why the key is dim and small in Mephisto's hands but comes to light and life in Faust's has been ingeniously and convincingly explained by several commentators, though always abstractly, conceptually. What follows here is intended not as a replacement but as a supplement, particularly for bringing the whole matter over from the metaphysical to the symbolic realm. One of the prominent works on Renaissance symbolism, Picinelli's *Mondo Simbolico*, which I used in the edition of 1670, can help show us the way. On examining his article on "Chiave" one can see quite clearly that neither we nor Goethe had to wait for Freud or his followers to explicate the sexual connotations of the key symbol (it was only the dichotomous, idealistic-materialistic nineteenth century that obscured the issue). Picinelli, after his allusive though obvious explication of this basic meaning, goes on to interpret it in its wider connotations as the indication of the ineffable, overwhelming yearning of man for the ultimate in mind and emotions.—In sum, the key opens up the way to the realm of the Mothers and brings back with it the creative, vaticinatory tripod, by means of which the poet, the creator, can transcend the limits of time and place. In this scene, as variously in *Faust*, from the initial "Dedication" onward, the mystery of the world of time and place and phenomena is central.

Let us then look more closely at the Janus symbol for its further connotative associations to the Faust drama. There is probably no better approach than through one of the favorite poets of Goethe's youth—Ovid—albeit through a work that few but specialists would care to read. And yet, near the beginning of the *Fasti*, that technical work on the Roman calendar, comes the splendid poetic passage on the apparition of Janus to the poet, a passage that will hold the attention of anyone who chances to glance into the work. Here is probably the closest poetic parallel to the apparition of the Earth Spirit in Faust's first scene. Even though the differences are more striking than the similarities (Ovid, for example, is better at managing the conversation than Faust), tension, tone, and situation establish the relationship as do certain features of Janus' description of his nature and function. The poet invokes "Janus, opener of the softly gliding year," and wonders about his attributes:

*While thus I mused, the tablets in my hand, methought the house
grew brighter than it was before. Then of a sudden sacred Janus, in
his two-headed shape, offered his double visage to my wondering eyes.
A terror seized me, I felt my hair stiffen with fear, and with a sudden
chill my bosom froze. He, holding in his right hand his staff and in
his left the key, to me these accents uttered from his front mouth:
"Dismiss thy fear, thy answer take, laborious singer of the days, and
mark my words. The ancients called me Chaos, for a being from of
old am I; observe the long, long ages of which my song shall tell.
Yon lucid air and the three other bodies, fire, water, earth, were
huddled all in one. When once, through the discord of its elements,
the mass parted, dissolved, and went in diverse ways to seek new
homes, flame sought the height, air filled the nearer space, while earth
and sea sank in the middle deep. 'Twas then that I, till that time a
mere ball, a shapeless lump, assumed the face and members of a god.
And even now, small index of my erst chaotic state, my front and
back look just the same. Now hear the other reason for the shape you
ask about, that you may know it and my office too. Whate'er you see
anywhere—sky, sea, clouds, earth—all things are closed and opened
by my hand. The guardianship of this vast universe is in my hands
alone, and none but me may rule the wheeling pole. When I choose
to send forth peace from tranquil halls, she freely walks the ways
unhindered. But with blood and slaughter the whole world would
welter, did not the bars unbending hold the barricadoed wars. I sit
at heaven's gate with the gentle Hours; my office regulates the goings
and the comings of Jupiter himself. Hence Janus is my name. . . ."*[39]

To return to the bas-relief, the important thing for Goethe's creative
imagination is not its specific content (certainly not any ideological content)
but, above all, the general configuration, the general mood impinging upon the
beholder, especially from the middle region where, with the consent of heaven
above, the earthly transitory below is transmuted into divine permanence
through the power of the creative arts. Though the "Apotheosis of Homer" is
a late work, and Goethe himself pointed out the signs of decline in it, he still
recognized its merits and saw on it the unmistakable stamp of a great artistic
tradition. If one looks at the goddesses here depicted, one is struck by a certain
enigmatic quality which affects us again and again in the presence of works
of ancient art, a kind of divine detachment. The several Muses seem to be
standing and sitting there in a state of trance-like reverie, "in sich versunken,"

remote from any concern with the world of phenomena, and yet at the same time presiding over its efforts to rise from impermanence to permanence, from mortality to immortality. To this singular mood which many an ancient work induces in the beholder, Goethe himself bears witness. Fortunately, he does so with specific reference also to the group of the Muses as it occurs in ancient art, and that in the late 1790's, when his Roman years lay behind him and this particular work was living in him as a transmuted memory rather than as a concrete presence. As a result, his basic, subconscious reaction is revealed with the factors that could be assimilated into his mytho-poetic processes. In his essay "Über Laokoon" he observes by way of contrast:

> A Jupiter with a thunder bolt on his lap, a Juno reposing in her majesty and womanly dignity, a Minerva lost in introspection are objects that, so to speak, have no relation outward, they rest upon and in themselves, they are the first, dearest objects of the art of sculpture. Yet in the glorious round of the mythical circle of art in which the separate independent natures stand and rest, there are smaller circles where the separate figures are conceived and fashioned in relation to one another. For example, the nine Muses with their leader Apollo: each is conceived and carried out for her own sake, and yet in the whole manifold choir she becomes even more interesting.[40]

In a contemporaneous essay, "Über die Gegenstände der bildenden Kunst," "On the Subjects of Pictorial Art," he offers a significant variant on these remarks:

> To be sure, there can be a particular circle, a cycle of bodies which together, so to speak, constitute a mystical body, like the nine Muses with Apollo.[41]

This can serve as an indication of the kind of emotional and imaginative impact the bas-relief and related images made on Goethe, and the train of associations it released in him.

To this point I had worked only with the modern illustration of the bas-relief to be found in the valuable and convenient work by Max Wegner, *Goethes Anschauung antiker Kunst* (1944). Several years ago a happy chance put into my hands a fine copy of the Cuperus with the folded engraving of the "Apotheosis" and all the other plates present and in good condition. Typically for the learned work of the time, there is a great elaboration of minute philological detail, but there is also a rich collection of connotative passages from ancient writers. In the section on MNHMH, Cuperus does extend the meaning of a brief quotation from Athenaeus. He cites memory as preserving "the ancient order of things of the Greeks" and comments that it truly also has brought forth the ancient voices and has, so to speak, recalled many of the dead to the light.[42]

However, the real reward came in one of the appended studies, not so much the one on the Gemma Augustaea, with its Augustus and boy charioteer, as the one on inscriptions, of which the second part is concerned with inscriptions to the Mothers, the Matres Deae (pp. 264–71). Though the classic references to Diodorus Siculus, Plutarch, and others are given, the chief concern is with the transalpine monuments with inscriptions bearing witness to the cult of the Mothers in the northern provinces of the Roman Empire. Cuperus offers evidence that the cult of the Mothers was not limited to Britain, as John Selden had claimed. In addition to the printed inscriptions, there is an engraved illustration of one of the monuments with an epigraph and above it a bas-relief of three Mother goddesses enthroned. This makes it a matter of certainty that the connotative bridge from Mnemosyne and the Muses to the Mothers was actually made for Goethe at this time.

Though it will never be possible to trace with certainty the poetic processes that culminated in Goethe's creation of the myth of the Mothers, we do now have a better point of departure in the wealth of cognate images and configurations that came to the poet in the course of a long life. What we do know now is the complex of myth and story out of which his creation grew, even though the exact lines of tradition and development can never be determined with finality. What is more, we also become aware of previously unnoticed filiations and symbolic relations to other scenes in *Faust*.

To summarize: The vital nucleus of the whole creation was probably the perilous voyage outside normal place and time which the hero traditionally undertakes for some high purpose. Then, of necessity, a decision had to be made as to the kind of supernatural region to which the hero goes. The earlier, more conventional decision was for a journey to the realm of Persephone to recover Helen. This was relegated behind the scenes and yielded dramatic precedence to a more unusual kind of voyage, completely beyond place and time, to the creative matrix of the forms which issue forth into the reality of place and time and return again. We know now that such a realm existed in poetic tradition, in varied manifestation in the myth of Claudianus, with important elements also in Ariosto's *Orlando Furioso*, Tasso's *Jerusalem Delivered*, and elsewhere in the poetic and mythic tradition still alive in Goethe, though partly lost soon thereafter. The third major element is the Orphic-Delphic, the initiation into the mysteries—this achieved, after preliminary instruction, through a solemn, awesome progress in the course of which is revealed, in symbol but also as indelible experience, the ultimate mystery of life: in birth, death, and rebirth. *Omnia mutantur, nihil interit.* A Persephone scene, however moving, would have had far less resonance, far less filiation extending to every part of the drama and unifying it under the great vision of creativity. It would also have had far less power to haunt the minds and imaginations of men to ever renewed effort to penetrate the veil of mystery with which Goethe surrounded this episode and related scenes. It may be possible to trace the creative genesis of the myth of the Mothers, to know what it consists of, but the veil of mystery cannot and should not be drawn away.

There may, however, still be serious misgivings on one fundamental point: Did Goethe's creative poetic mind really work this way? Would he or could he, in the fire of his poetic imagination, have fused all these widely divergent, albeit interrelated myths and images into this unified, integral, intense creation? Do not the results before us postulate an entirely different process of creation? In another kind of poet perhaps yes, but as for Goethe, he himself declared that he achieved his poetic synthesis in the very way suggested in this study. He did this quite clearly in the important conversation with Eckermann about *Faust* on May 6, 1827, quoted in Chapter One, and also in his essay of 1823, "Bedeutende Fördernis durch ein einziges geistreiches Wort," "Significant Advancement through a Single Sagacious Word":

> *What has been said about my objective thinking I should also like equally to apply to an objective poetry. Certain great motifs, legends, ancient historical traditions made such a deep impression on my mind that I preserved them forty to fifty years vivid and effective within myself. I felt it my fondest possession to find such precious images often renewed in my imagination, where, to be sure, they were in a constant state of transformation and yet, remaining intrinsically unchanged, ripened toward a purer form, a more definite representation.*[43]

Fortunately, Goethe did more than describe his particular kind of creative process; he also gave valuable suggestions for the understanding of a work created in this manner. In the letter to Iken of September 23, 1827, just at the time of his studies for the "Apotheosis of Homer," he wrote with reference to the recently published Helena act:

> *In such hope for a discerning participation I let myself go completely in the composition of the "Helena," without thinking of any public or any single reader, convinced that whoever readily grasps and understands the whole will also gradually with loving patience come into possession of the details. . . . With regard also to other obscure passages in earlier and later works I should like to call the following to mind: since so much from our experiences cannot be plainly stated and directly communicated, I have long since chosen the method of revealing the more hidden meaning to the attentive by means of*

images placed in juxtaposition to one another and, so to speak, mutually reflecting one another.[44]

The contextual method I have ventured to use in this investigation seems to be a close approximation to the approach that Goethe here advocates. My contention has been that this scene, if it is not to remain totally ambiguous (as it has been under isolated study from discrepant ideological approaches), must be studied in the context of the drama as a whole and in the even larger context of the main configurations of this scene as they occur elsewhere in Goethe's own work and in the relevant cultural heritage that stood at his command. In this way the necessary transillumination will be provided.

In the course thus pursued, in the interpretation thus developed, the whole episode remains pure myth and symbol, as the poet no doubt intended it to be. A reduction to philosophic or allegorical terms casts a blight over it, inevitably, and leaves only the skeleton of a living creation. Similarly, an interpretation in post-Goethean terms, anthropological or psychological, in all the range from Bachofen through Freud to Jung, including the subjectivist projectionists, just as inevitably introduces anachronisms and scurrilities. One may well except those features in Jung which are in the continuum of the primary tradition. But why not simply stay with the primary tradition? Why put distorting and discoloring lenses between oneself and the phenomena, instead of observing them directly against their organic and sufficient background? A moderately sensitive reading will show that Goethe knew very well what it was all about and so did the ancients he read and revered; it will show how clear and plain-spoken they actually were. It is only the direct comparison of the texts that reveals, for example, that Goethe endowed Mephisto-Phorkias with aspects of Demeter, and Helen with aspects of Persephone as well as Euridice, and it becomes clear almost at once why he did so. For those who can think in images instead of merely conceptually, one need simply note that Faust had just previously appeared in the masque as Plutus, god of wealth, son of Demeter, and therefore brother of Persephone, that in one tradition Persephone's son was Dionysus, that Faust's son Euphorion is described as "faunenartig," and that Euphorion's early childhood is brought into explicit parallel to that of Hermes.

In the end though, with or without modern explications, the final mystery will not be laid bare. And Goethe tells us why it will not be, in a passage of his wonderfully gently penetrating essay, "Bildung und Umbildung,"

"Formation and Transformation," which is as applicable to poetic nature as it is to organic nature:

> *As we contemplate such a wondrous structure and better learn to perceive how it arises, we again come upon an important principle of organization: that no life can be effective on a surface and there exert its productive power, that, on the contrary, all of life activity requires a covering that will preserve its delicate entity against the rough outer environment . . . so that it may fulfill what its intrinsic nature calls for. . . . Everything that is to be vitally effective must be enveloped.*[45]

¹ "Das sogenannte Aus-Sich-Schöpfen macht gewöhnlich falsche Originale und Manieristen." Johann Wolfgang Goethe, *Maximen und Reflexionen*, ed. Max Hecker (hereafter referred to as Hecker), Schriften der Goethe-Gesellschaft, vol. 21 (Weimar: 1907) p. 232, no. 1119.

"Egon Ebert . . . hätte sich sollen an die Überlieferung der Chronik halten, da hätte aus seinem Gedicht etwas werden können. Wenn ich bedenke, wie Schiller die Überlieferung studierte, was er sich für Mühe mit der Schweiz gab, als er seinen Tell schrieb, und wie Shakespeare die Chroniken benutzte und ganze Stellen daraus wörtlich in seine Stücke aufgenommen hat, so könnte man einem jetzigen jungen Dichter auch wohl dergleichen zumuten. In meinem Clavigo habe ich aus den Memoiren des Beaumarchais ganze Stellen." *Goethes Gespräche*, ed. Flodoard von Biedermann (hereafter referred to as Biedermann), 5 vols. (Leipzig 1909–11), 4:103 (with Eckermann, April 10, 1829).

² "Dieser [Mephistopheles], der nicht bekennen mag, daß er im klassischen Hades nichts zu sagen habe. . . ." Goethe's draft of an introduction to the Helena drama, dated December 17, 1826. See Hans Gerhard Gräf, *Goethe über seine Dichtungen*, (hereafter referred to as Gräf) pt. 2, vol. 2 (Frankfurt, 1904), p. 365. See also Chapter Eight.

³ Unfortunately, not one of the earlier translations of *Faust II* available to me could be used for the present purpose. Just at those points where precise English equivalents are essential, the extant renderings are, at best, too free, at worst, quite misleading. Unfortunately also, none of them sounds quite right when read aloud. The primary purpose of the present version is to offer as close an equivalent as possible to the German original (including the rendering of ambiguities neutrally, without taking sides interpretatively). This, however, brings with it the obligation to strive for as comparable a poetic and imaginative level as the adverse circumstances of translation will permit. To what an extent this was attainable, here and in the poetic passages that follow, only a comparison with earlier translations will show. With unlimited time for polishing and recasting, continuing improvement would, no doubt, be possible.

⁴ "Es war im ganzen . . . nicht meine Art, als Poet nach Verkörperung von etwas Abstraktem zu streben. Ich empfing in meinem Innern Eindrücke, und zwar Eindrücke sinnlicher, lebensvoller, lieblicher, bunter, hundertfältiger Art, wie eine rege Einbildungskraft es mir darbot; und ich hatte als Poet weiter nichts zu tun, als solche Anschauungen und Eindrücke in mir künstlerisch zu ründen und auszubilden und durch eine lebendige Darstellung so zum Vorschein zu bringen, daß andere dieselbigen Eindrücke erhielten, wenn sie mein Dargestelltes hörten oder lasen." Biedermann, 3:394 to Eckermann, May 6, 1827.

See also the immediately preceding passage for Goethe's clear denial that the *Faust* could be approached in an ideological, philosophical manner. See also note 43 below for a parallel statement from Goethe's writings on his poetic creative processes.

[5] "Genau aber genommen, so ist nichts theatralisch, als was für die Augen zugleich symbolisch ist: eine wichtige Handlung, die auf eine noch wichtigere deutet." In "Shakespeare und kein Ende," *Goethes Werke. Herausgegeben im Auftrage der Großherzogin Sophie von Sachsen*, Weimar, 1887 ff. (hereafter referred to as W.A., with a roman division number followed by arabic volume and page numbers) I, 41:66–67. Similarly, Biedermann, 3:280 (to Eckermann, July 26, 1826).

Among Goethe's other reflections and definitions concerned with the symbol and the symbolic, the following may serve in supplement:

"Es ist ein großer Unterschied, ob der Dichter zum Allgemeinen das Besondere sucht oder im Besondern das Allgemeine schaut. Aus jener Art entsteht Allegorie, wo das Besondere nur als Beispiel, als Exempel des Allgemeinen gilt; die letztere aber ist eigentlich die Natur der Poesie, sie spricht ein Besonderes aus, ohne ans Allgemeine zu denken oder darauf hinzuweisen. Wer nun dieses Besondere lebendig faßt, erhält zugleich das Allgemeine mit, ohne es gewahr zu werden, oder erst spät." Hecker, p. 53, no. 279.

"Das ist die wahre Symbolik, wo das Besondere das Allgemeinere repräsentiert, nicht als Traum und Schatten, sondern als lebendig-augenblickliche Offenbarung des Unerforschlichen." *Ibid.*, p. 59, no. 314. See also p. 230 f., nos., 1112 and 1113.

[6] Harold Jantz, "The Symbolic Prototypes of Faust the Ruler," *Wächter und Hüter. Festschrift für Hermann J. Weigand*, eds. Curt von Faber du Faur, Konstantin Reichardt, and Heinz Bluhm (New Haven, 1957), pp. 77–91.

[7] Harold Jantz, "Kontrafaktur, Montage, Parodie: Tradition und symbolische Erweiterung," in *Tradition und Ursprünglichkeit, Akten des III. Internationalen Germanistenkongresses 1965 in Amsterdam*, eds. Werner Kohlschmidt and Herman Meyer (Bern and Munich, 1966), pp. 53–65.

[8] Claudius Claudianus, *De Consulatu Stilichonis*, II, 424–445. Trans. Maurice Platnauer (Loeb Classical Library, London, 1922), 2:33–35.

[9] "Wir gingen neulich, mein Gemahl und ich, in dem Hain jenseits des Cocytus, wo, wie du weißt, die Gestalten der Träume sich lebhaft darstellen und hören lassen." W.A. I, 38:16.

[10] W.A. I, 38:379–82. There is general agreement, confirmed by internal and external evidence, that Goethe was the author of this anonymous review.

[11] See, e.g., plates D, F, G, N, and especially M, the lower relief, which is reproduced in this volume.

[12] Gräf, 338. This earlier, briefer draft is dated June 10, 1826.

[13] *Ibid.*, 372. "So gelangen sie abwärts bis an den Fuß des Olympus; hier stoßen sie auf eine lange Prozession von Sibyllen, an Zahl weit mehr als zwölfe. Chiron schildert die ersten vorüberziehenden als alte Bekannte und empfiehlt seinen Schützling der sinnigen, wohldenkenden Tochter des Tiresias, Manto." This draft is dated December 17, 1826.

[14] "Ich kann Ihnen weiter nichts verraten . . ., als daß ich beim Plutarch gefunden, daß im griechischen Altertume von Müttern als Gottheiten die Rede gewesen. Dies ist alles,

was ich der Überlieferung verdanke, das übrige ist meine eigene Erfindung." Biedermann 4:188.

[15] See note 6, "The Symbolic Prototypes," pp. 87–89.

[16] On the "Paria" and other works see his essay, "Bedeutende Fördernis durch ein einziges geistreiches Wort," W.A. II, 11:60. On the Helena Act, see his various statements, e.g., the letter to Sulpiz Boisserée, October 22, 1826 (Gräf, 350) and to Nees von Esenbeck, May 25, 1827 (Gräf, 397).

[17] What follows is largely a briefer reformulation for present purposes of "The Place of the 'Eternal-Womanly' in Goethe's Faust Drama," *PMLA*, 68 (1953): 791–805.

[18] W.A. I, 49^1:325 "Denn wie wir sonst auf heiligen Bildern um das Haupt der verklärten Mutter Gottes Kreise von Engelsköpfchen sehen, die sich nach und nach in glänzende Wölkchen auflösen, ebenso ist es hier mit den Rosen gemeint, zu welchen die rot gesäumten Wölkchen der Morgendämmerung bedeutungsvoll gestaltet sind. . . .

Wenn um das Götterkind Auroren
In Finsternis werden Rosen geboren.

[19] Most familiar perhaps are the passages in his review of *Die schönen Künste* by Johann Georg Sulzer (W.A. I, 37:208–10) and Werther's reflections in the letter of August 18 (W.A. I, 19:73–76). In the latter, especially, the ancient tradition of the ominous dual aspect of nature, as fruitful womb and darksome grave, is eloquently expressed.

[20] "Das Wahre, mit dem Göttlichen identisch, läßt sich niemals von uns direkt erkennen, wir schauen es nur im Abglanz, im Beispiel, Symbol, in einzelnen und verwandten Erscheinungen; wir werden es gewahr als unbegreifliches Leben und können dem Wunsch nicht entsagen, es dennoch zu begreifen." W.A. II, 12:74.

[21] See note 14 above. In addition to the passage from the Marcellus biography (ch. 20) to be examined, another Plutarch passage, from the dialogue on the cessation of the oracles (ch. 22), is occasionally cited. It is worth quoting here since it has some relevance to our larger concerns and did enter into the general literary tradition about a mysterious realm where all that has been and will be is preserved. The speaker, Cleombrotus, is reporting the opinions of a mysterious stranger from the Erythrian Sea, who is later identified as a Dorian Greek, the son of Petron of Himera who had written a little book on the subject. He differed from Plato who "summarily decided against an infinite number of worlds, but had doubts about a limited number . . ., for himself, he kept to one." The stranger "said that the worlds are not infinite in number, nor one, nor five, but one hundred and eighty-three, arranged in the form of a triangle, each side of the triangle having sixty worlds; of the three left over each is placed at an angle, and those that are next to one another are in contact and revolve gently as in a dance. The inner area of the triangle is the common hearth of all, and is called the Plain of Truth, in which the accounts, the forms, and the patterns of all things that have come to pass and of all that shall come to pass rest undisturbed; and round about them lies Eternity, whence Time, like an ever-flowing stream, is conveyed to the worlds. Opportunity to see and to contemplate these things is vouchsafed to human souls once in ten thousand years if they have lived goodly lives; and the best of the initiatory rites here are but a dream of that highest rite and initiation. . . ." The translation is that of Frank Cole Babbitt, *Plutarch's Moralia*, V, 415–17 (Loeb Classical Library, London, 1936).

[22] See Elise von Keudell, *Goethe als Benutzer der Weimarer Bibliothek* (Weimar, 1931), p. 129, no. 802. Goethe's last diary entry about the work, on December 26 reads, "Diodor von Sicilien Bd. 2" (W.A. III, 4:356). Since volume two goes through book five, this means that he probably read the section (IV:79–80) concerned with the Mothers at this time.

[23] Harold Jantz, "The Function of the 'Walpurgis Night's Dream' in the Faust Drama," *Monatshefte* 44 (1952): 397–408, esp. p. 408.

[24] Vergil, *Georgics* IV, 363–67, 391–93, 495–98, trans. H. Rushton Fairclough (Loeb Classical Library, London and New York, 1927), pp. 221–31.

[25] Ariosto, *Orlando Furioso*, canto 35, stanza 18, trans. Allan Gilbert, 2 vols. (New York, 1954) II, 2:612. The example here given is of the old man who is the equivalent of time on earth, and produces like effects. In Goethe's earlier plan for a Persephone scene there are "drei Richter," "in deren ehernes Gedächtnis sich alles einsenkt, was in dem Lethestrome zu ihren Füßen vorüberrollend zu verschwinden scheint." (Gräf, 373–74.)

[26] *The Homeric Hymns*, trans. Andrew Lang (New York and London, 1899) pp. 189–90, 193–94, 209–10.

[27] "Das Gebildete wird sogleich wieder umgebildet, und wir haben uns, wenn wir einigermaßen zum lebendigen Anschaun der Natur gelangen wollen, selbst so beweglich und bildsam zu erhalten, nach dem Beispiele, mit dem sie uns vorgeht." W.A. II, 6:10.

[28] "Wo der Naturforscher die Anfänge der Gestalten anfaßt.—Letzte Enden der Organisation.— Durchführung durch Bildung und Umbildung.— Bis zur menschlichen Gestalt im allgemeinen." W.A. I, 47:292.

[29] "Es entsteht nämlich, da so viel von Gestaltung und Umgestaltung gesprochen worden, die Frage, ob man denn wirklich die Schädelknochen aus Wirbelknochen ableiten und ihre anfängliche Gestalt, ohngeachtet so großer und entschiedener Veränderungen, noch anerkennen solle und dürfe." W.A. II, 8:135.

[30] W.A. I, 3:84. The poem first appeared without title in *Zur Morphologie*, 1820, third number, title page verso.

[31] See Gräf, 350 and 397. "Die 'Helena' ist eine meiner ältesten Konzeptionen, gleichzeitig mit 'Faust', immer nach Einem Sinne, aber immer um und um gebildet." "Wie vielfach hatte sich diese in langen, kaum übersehbaren Jahren gestaltet und umgestaltet."

[32] Cf., e.g., Karl Kerényi, *Das Agäische Fest* (Amsterdam, Leipzig: 1941), p. 72, and the references there to his earlier *Das göttliche Mädchen* and *Pythagoras und Orpheus*.
Kurt May, *Faust II. Teil in der Sprachform gedeutet* (Berlin: 1936), p. 67, e.g.: "Die Formgebung des Gesprächs der Mütterszene . . . muß letztlich aus dem *faustischen* Welt- und Lebensverständnis heraus begriffen werden, dem Mephisto hier bis zu äußerster Verleugnung seines innersten Wesens dient." To be sure, where May tries to intellectualize and explicate the phenomena he has correctly observed, we must hesitate to follow him in such rationalizations.

[33] "Helena gehört dem Orkus und kann durch Zauberkünste wohl herausgelockt, aber nicht festgehalten werden." "Helena erscheint: durch einen magischen Ring ist ihr die Körperlichkeit wieder gegeben." Gräf, 236.

[34] "Bei einem großen Feste an des deutschen Kaisers Hof werden Faust und

Mephistopheles aufgefordert, eine Geistererscheinung zu bewirken; ungern zwar, aber gedrängt rufen sie die verlangten Idole von Helena und Paris hervor." Gräf, 364.

"Faust aus einer schweren, langen Schlafsucht, während welcher seine Träume sich vor den Augen des Zuschauers sichtbar umständlich begeben, ins Leben zurückgerufen, tritt exaltiert hervor und fordert, von dem höchsten Anschauen ganz durchdrungen, den Besitz heftig von Mephistopheles. Dieser, der nicht bekennen mag, daß er im klassischen Hades nichts zu sagen habe, auch dort nicht einmal gern gesehen sei, bedient sich seines früheren probaten Mittels, seinen Gebieter nach allen Seiten hin und her zu sprengen. . . ." Gräf, 365.

[35] Von Keudell, *Goethe als Benutzer*, p. 298, no. 1877, with accurate title but without reference to the anonymous English translator. The Thomas Taylor translation, though not as accurate as the more modern one by W. H. S. Jones and H. A. Ormerod (Loeb Classical Library, London and New York: 1918 ff.), serves the present purpose well enough despite its various smaller and greater lapses. In compensation, there remains the matter of the elaborate notes appended to volume III, some of which touch on central interests of Goethe and contain neoplatonic extensions of mythological concerns nowhere else available to him at that time. The Trophonius account occurs in Pausanias IX, 39 (III, 92–95).

A further indication of Goethe's long familiarity with the subject matter of the Trophonius oracle is contained in his letters to Philipp Seidel just before and during his Italian stay, from August 13 and September 2, 1786, and January 13, 1787. He had lent Karl August the libretto of an opera, *La Grotta di Trofonio*, and now Count Harach had promised to send him the score from Vienna. Writing from Rome on January 13, he not only mentioned the opera again but also varied the familiar ancient saying about the oracle to express his feelings about Rome: "Wie man sagt, daß einer nicht wieder froh wird, der ein Gespenst gesehn hat, so möchte ich sagen, daß einer, der Italien besonders Rom recht gesehn hat, nie ganz in seinem Gemüte unglücklich werden kann."

There is no evidence, though there is of course some likelihood, that Goethe knew an earlier Viennese opera that made use of the traditional motif of a mysterious realm in which all time reposes. It was written by Metastasio and set to music by Fux, and in its title already indicates its main sources of inspiration in the *Aeneid*, book six, and in Claudianus: *Enea negli Elisi, overo il Tempio dell' Eternità*, 1731. One brief quotation from the stage directions at the transformation scene will serve to indicate the nature of this realm (B1ʳ): "Si vede . . . il tempio dell' Eternità sostenuto da colonne trasparenti, fra le quali saranno ordinatamente disposte le imagini delle Eroine, e degli Eroi dall'antichità più celebrati. Sederà nel mezzo l'Eternità. A' lati di lei la Virtù, e la Gloria. Più basso il Tempo."

[36] "Er aber, in seiner gewöhnlichen Art hüllte sich in Geheimnisse, indem er mich mit großen Augen anblickte und mir die Worte wiederholte: "Die Mütter! Mütter! 's klingt so wunderlich!" Biedermann IV, 188.

[37] "Klar ist . . . die . . . abgebildete göttliche Verehrung Homers auf dem untern Teile des Bildes. . . .

"Auf der Höhe des Bergs Zeus sitzend . . . Mnemosyne hat eben von ihm die Erlaubnis zur Vergötterung ihres Lieblings erhalten . . . die Mutter alles Dichtens. . . .

"Eine jüngere Muse, kindlich munter hinabspringend, verkündets freudig ihren sieben Schwestern, welche, auf den beiden mittleren Planen sitzend und stehend, mit dem, was oben vorging, beschäftigt scheinen. Sodann erblickt man eine Höhle, da Apollo Musagetes in herkömmlich langem Sängerkleide. . . .

"Von oben herein wird nämlich das göttliche Patent erteilt und den beiden mittleren Reihen publiziert; das unterste, vierte . . . Feld aber stellt die wirkliche, obgleich poetisch-symbolische Verleihung der zugestandenen hohen Ehre dar.

"Problematisch bleiben uns jedoch noch zwei Figuren in dem rechten Winkel der zweiten Reihe von unten. Auf einem Piedestal steht eine Figur . . . eines . . . Mannes von mittlerem Alter. . . . in der Rechten hält er eine Papier- oder Pergamentrolle, und über seinem Haupte zeigt sich der obere Teil eines Dreifußes. . . ." W.A. I, 49^2:26–28.

In a preliminary draft of the essay Goethe mentions the late origin of the work: "Daß es später ist, zeigt schon die mehr als sonst im Altertum gebräuchliche Allegorie, hier sogar durch Inschriften verdeutlicht." *Ibid.*, 259.

[38] "So ist ihm [einem Schauspieler], . . . durchaus nötig, daß er die auf uns gekommenen antiken Bildwerke wohl studiert und sich die ungesuchte Grazie ihres Sitzens, Stehens und Gehens wohl eingeprägt habe." Biedermann III, 362.

[39] Ovid, *Fasti*, I, 93–127, trans. Sir James George Frazer (London, 1929), pp. 6–9.

[40] "Ein Jupiter mit einem Donnerkeil im Schoß, eine Juno, die auf ihrer Majestät und Frauenwürde ruht, eine in sich versenkte Minerva sind Gegenstände, die gleichsam nach außen keine Beziehung haben, sie ruhen auf und in sich und sind die ersten, liebsten Gegenstände der Bildhauerkunst. Aber in dem herrlichen Zirkel des mythischen Kunstkreises, in welchem die einzelnen selbständigen Naturen stehen und ruhen, gibt es kleinere Zirkel, wo die einzelnen Gestalten in Bezug auf andere gedacht und gearbeitet sind. Z. E. die neun Musen mit ihrem Führer Apoll, ist jede für sich gedacht und ausgeführt, aber in dem ganzen mannigfaltigen Chor wird sie noch interessanter." W.A. I, 47:105.

[41] "Nun kann es aber einen gewissen Kreis, einen Zyklus von Gegenständen geben, die zusammen gleichsam einen mystischen Gegenstand ausmachen, wie die neun Musen mit dem Apoll. . . ." *Ibid.*, 92.

[42] *Apotheosis vel Consecratio Homeri*, Amstelodami, 1683, p. 104: ". . . non modo Memoria recte illi tribuitur, qua teste Athenaeo conservavit τὴν ἀρχαιαν τῶν Ἑλλήνων κατάστασιν, verum etiam quia memoriae prodidit voces priscas, multasque veluti mortuas revocavit in lucem." Cuperus in reference gives only "Lib. 14" in the margin. Since Goethe early and late read the *Deipnosophistae*, one is impelled to search through the long fourteenth book in hope of finding more of relevance. When one at last finds the little quotation (627e), one gains no further enlightenment, but only renewed amusement at what can be done with a quotation out of context.

[43] "Was nun von meinem gegenständlichen Denken gesagt ist, mag ich wohl auch ebenmäßig auf eine gegenständliche Dichtung beziehen. Mir drückten sich gewisse große Motive, Legenden, uraltgeschichtlich Überliefertes so tief in den Sinn, daß ich sie vierzig bis fünfzig Jahre lebendig und wirksam im Innern erhielt; mir schien der schönste Besitz, solche werte Bilder oft in der Einbildungskraft erneut zu sehen, da sie sich denn zwar immer umgestalteten, doch, ohne sich zu verändern, einer reineren Form, einer entschiednern Darstellung entgegenreiften." W.A. II, 11:60.

[44] "In solchen Hoffnungen einsichtiger Teilnahme habe ich bei Ausarbeitung der 'Helena' mich ganz gehen lassen, ohne an irgend ein Publikum noch an einen einzelnen Leser

zu denken, überzeugt daß, wer das Ganze leicht ergreift und faßt, mit liebevoller Geduld sich auch nach und nach das Einzelne zueignen werde. . . .

Auch wegen anderer dunkler Stellen in frühern und spätern Gedichten möchte ich Folgendes zu bedenken geben. Da sich manches unserer Erfahrungen nicht rund aussprechen und direkt mitteilen läßt, so habe ich seit langem das Mittel gewählt, durch einander gegenübergestellte und sich gleichsam in einander abspiegelnde Gebilde, den geheimeren Sinn dem Aufmerkenden zu offenbaren." (Gräf, 413–14.)

[45] "Wie wir nun einen solchen Wunderbau betrachten und die Art, wie er hervorsteigt, näher einsehen lernen, so begegnet uns abermals ein wichtiger Grundsatz der Organisation: daß kein Leben auf einer Oberfläche wirken und daselbst seine hervorbringende Kraft äußern könne, sondern die ganze Lebenstätigkeit verlangt eine Hülle, die gegen das äußere rohe Element . . . ihr zartes Wesen bewahre, damit sie das, was ihrem Innern spezifisch obliegt, vollbringe. . . . alles, was lebendig wirken soll, muß eingehüllt sein." (W.A. II, 6:14.)

Designed by Gerard A. Valerio

Composed in Weiss Roman
by Monotype Composition Company

Printed offset by Universal Lithographers, Inc.
on 60 lb. Warren's 1854

Bound by L. H. Jenkins, Inc.